How To Get Started In Christian Music

By Chris Christian

Edited by John Styll

Home Sweet Home
PUBLICATIONS
Dallas, Texas

How To Get Started In Christian Music
Copyright © 1986 Chris Christian
A Division of Home Sweet Home Publications
P.O. Box 202406
Dallas, Texas 75220

ISBN 0-9616817-0-5

Printed in the United States of America.

Table of Contents

Table of Contents

How To Get Started In Christian Music

P eople frequently ask me, "How do I get started in Christian music?" Although the steps will be different for each of us, this book offers valuable insights as well as practical guidelines that will help you answer this and other related questions.

Chris Christian has been in this business almost since "contemporary Christian music" became an industry of its own. Consequently, he has a great deal of first-hand experience from which to address the questions of a beginning artist or songwriter.

One ingredient common to all of us should be our seeking direction from the Lord. My wish for you is that, with much prayer, He will make your calling clear and open the proper doors.

May He direct your search.

Amy Grant

How To Get Started In Christian Music

This book is dedicated to my wife Shanon who, for six years, unselfishly allowed our meals to be surrounded by business, our home to be a hotel, and our private lives to be put on hold for "later on." Her love and her support of my calling and my goals are what made my schedule possible.

I will never know how she continually found more of herself to give at times when it seemed she was about to break.

I am thankful to my Creator for keeping us together through our stormiest seas and for giving us a family. Now much of the time that used to be focused in the studio is focused on them.

To you, dear reader, I hope this book gives a great deal of direction in your Christian ministry. Above all, though, put God, your family, and your loved ones first. Then, and only then, will you reap a worthwhile harvest.

Chris

How To Get Started In Christian Music

T he very fact that you are reading this preface indicates to me that you feel the Lord has blessed you—or someone you know—with a talent you would like to use for Him. It is for my talented brothers and sisters that I wrote this book, and I did so for several reasons. First, I want to show you how Christian music has gotten to where it is today and who was involved in the journey. I also hope to help you determine whether you have potential for and a calling to a local, regional, or national ministry and what steps to take to pursue each one. I will also suggest ways to make your talents known to the right people as you seek to use that talent to God's glory.

How To Get Started In Christian Music

A young Christian songwriter walked up to a well-known artist after his performance and told the artist that the Lord had given him a song that he wanted to sing for the artist. The artist graciously listened to the whole song. At the close of the song, the artist thought to himself with a smile — "I can see why the Lord wanted to give that song away!"

Artistic quality in itself is almost impossible to judge. What one person feels is excellent, another might deem only mediocre. Determining a song's value becomes even more difficult in light of the fact that the Lord can use any song He chooses for a specific purpose.

In fact, any company, publisher, or producer who unequivocally tells a Christian that his or her song, voice, or talent cannot be used for the Lord underestimates the Lord's ability to use a willing heart. After all, each one of us is a weak vessel. Besides, often God will use most the person whose calling exceeds his talent.

At the same time, though, every talented Christian must not assume that he is destined to use this talent on a national scale. While it is very important to take your talent as far as the Lord sees fit, it is equally important to be content with a local or regional ministry if that is what He has called you to. Careful self-evaluation is required here. Each of us must examine our motives and set aside pride and ego so that we can be available for whatever work God has for us. Forget about sales charts, magazine covers, and sold-out concert halls. Concentrate instead on finding out what God's calling to *you* is.

My hope is that this book will help you do just that.

CHAPTER ONE

Christian Music
Then And Now

"Make a joyful noise unto the Lord"
—It's a call that dates back to
Old Testament times. Shepherd, King, and psalmist
David answered this call with beautiful songs, and he
could probably be considered the great-grandfather
of Christian music.

Throughout its history, the church has employed
hymns and sacred music in worship services. In
fact, many composers of classical music who are
revered today wrote music for the church hundreds
of years ago. Modern composers such as Ralph
Carmichael and Bill Gaither have updated some
of these hymns and set the stage for "inspirational"
or "middle of the road" (MOR) artists like Sandi
Patti.

While the roots of inspirational or traditional
Christian music can be traced back through church
history, contemporary Christian music goes back only
to the 1800s. After the Civil War, the black church
began to emerge. With it came a distinct brand of
music which became known as "spirituals." Rev.
Thomas A. Dorsey started calling them "gospel songs."
By the '40s and well into the '50s, black gospel had
its own record companies and radio programs.

Black gospel then gave rise to soul music. Gospel singers such as Sam Cooke and Ray Charles changed the lyrics and the gospel songs gained a wider audience. Sung with the same emotional intensity as gospel, the lyrics now dealt with earthly love.

At about the same time that black gospel was beginning to establish itself, white gospel singers began to organize themselves into groups of four people who would sing each note in a chord structure at one time. These quartets traveled to tent meetings or worship services singing simple, three- or four-chord songs of praise to our Lord and songs which dealt with such subjects as the Lord's return and our heavenly reward.

For many years, the most popular Christian music was performed by quartets or families such as The Stamps, The Florida Boys, The Blackwood Brothers, and the Imperials. These groups spent most of their time moving from town to town. Twice a year they would stop for three to five days to record a fast album to sell on the road.

A new music form—that good ol' rock 'n' roll—was born in the '50s. A white country boy from Memphis named Elvis Presley who had attended one of the city's black gospel churches began singing the kind of music he heard there on Sundays. Singing in this black gospel tradition, he set off a revolution in music which has forever changed our culture. From the rockabilly of the '50s to the British invasion of the '60s, rock 'n' roll has always made an indelible imprint on the younger generation.

Needless to say, the rock 'n' roll rage didn't catch on quite so quickly in the church. The classic hymns were the staple in nearly all white churches until the early '60s when Ray Repp introduced the folk mass

2

in some Catholic churches. Then in the mid-60s a "youth musical" called *Good News* emerged from the Southern Baptist Convention as their attempt to reach young people. A series of nondenominational musicals followed, many of which were written by Ralph Carmichael and Kurt Kaiser. While *Tell It Like It Is* and *Natural High* sound incredibly tame by today's standards, they were revolutionary at the time.

Contemporary Christian music, as we know it today, still didn't exist at the beginning of the '70s. In 1969 Larry Norman set the stage, though, when he recorded *Upon This Rock* for Capitol Records. This young singer/poet expressed his Christian convictions in rock music—a novel idea at the time.

While the Christian classic "I Wish We'd All Been Ready" came from that album, Larry's greatest contribution to Christian music was more than a particular song. Instead it was his example: he showed that scriptural ideas could be expressed in a musical form different from those of choirs and quartets. This precedent set, others began to express their thoughts, ideas, and praise to the Lord in their favorite musical styles. Two other well-known artists—Mylon LeFevre and John Fischer—also released their first Christian albums in 1969.

As the so-called "Jesus Movement" of the '70s swept across the country from the West Coast, more and more refugees from the counterculture of the '60s began to discover Christianity. These young people expressed their faith in the only musical idiom they knew—rock music. Calvary Chapel of Costa Mesa was a breeding ground for this new music. Groups such as Love Song, Children of the Day, The Way, and Mustard Seed Faith had their start at Calvary Chapel.

In 1972, Word Records established its Myrrh label and began to produce contemporary Christian music under the direction of Billy Ray Hearn (who left in 1976 to form Sparrow Records). Before long, new labels and groups were springing up everywhere. Since that time, contemporary Christian music has grown in quality as well as quantity, and it now accounts for well over half of all Christian music sales. (For a detailed history of today's Christian music, read *Contemporary Christain Music* by Paul Baker and published by Crossway Books.)

My own involvement in Christian music began when I was producing a pop/country group called Dogwood in Nashville, Tennessee. When Stan Moser of Word, Inc. in Waco, Texas heard the Dogwood album, he flew me down to Waco. Our meeting determined my career path for the next six years.

My initial production for Word was B.J. Thomas' first Christian album "Home Where I Belong". Having grown up listening to the harmonies and pop instrumentation of Bread and The Carpenters, I turned to these musical references when I wrote the songs for B.J.'s album. I also tried to model a few of the songs after his previous pop hits. ("Without a Doubt," for instance, was patterned after the song "Hooked on a Feeling" and "You Were There to Catch Me" after "Raindrops Keep Falling on My Head.") These songs probably helped introduce the idea that Christian lyrics could be sung either to a loved one or to God. Although today I feel that the message of such songs is too vague, they marked another developmental phase for many Christian artists and for contemporary Christian music itself.

4

While some good contemporary albums were recorded over the next few years, 1976 was a turning point. It was then that Brown Bannister, my engineer at the time, brought me a cassette of songs that a young, 16-year-old girl had written and put on tape. There was a very sincere, sweet, and innocent quality in her voice. Although I didn't know exactly what type of songs she should record, I couldn't shake the sense that there was something very appealing and believable about her.

I telephoned Stan Moser at Word and asked to produce an album for Amy Grant. They granted permission, and the rest of the story may well be the single most eloquent example of the Lord's hand on a project. From the very beginning, it seemed that nothing could stand in the way: again and again Amy has been given a platform to say the things the Lord wanted to say through her. To date, I have never known of a more dedicated artist or a faster rise in the Christian music field. Neither do I know of an artist who would be more deserving of such success.

One bit of information is worth mentioning here. Over a year and a half passed between finishing the album and the time when it was finally released. Looking back, I believe that the Lord was holding the album until Amy was mentally and spiritually ready for what was to happen. Take note, aspiring singers and songwriters. While God's timing can tax our patience, it can greatly increase our effectiveness.

So where is Christian Music going in the future? That is probably the most frequently asked question in Christian music circles today. Just as the Lord had His plan for Amy, only He knows how He will use music to spread His Word. I personally think the harp has to make a comeback one of these days! I think David would like that!

CHAPTER TWO

Christian Music — A Primer

Musical style aside, there are three basic types of Christain songs. First is the kind which edifies the listener and leads in worship. These worship and praise songs are "vertical" songs that can be sung either from the Lord's perspective or directly to the Lord.

Second is "horizontal" music which, as you might guess, lifts up brother to brother or sister to sister and deals with issues pertaining to our daily walk with the Lord. These songs can also deal with social or moral issues, especially in contemporary music.

Third are songs which are simply good, uplifting, entertaining songs written from a Christian perspective. While they may or may not mention Jesus or God by name, they make some statement about the Christian life.

Each kind of song has a distinct purpose and therefore is more appropriate for certain times and places than it is for others. In fact, someone once defined good music as that which is appropriate to its' intended purpose. A mellow praise song, for instance, can be just right for a Sunday morning worship service, but somehow out of place at many

Saturday night concerts. Likewise, most contemporary or rock music tends to be inappropriate in a worship service.

Still, much controversy rages in Christian circles about the purpose of today's music and about the artistic motives of those involved. A basic issue is whether Christian music is entertainment or ministry. I don't believe it to be an either/or, black or white proposition. In most cases, music can be both entertainment and ministry. Consider that to entertain is to divert one's attention and that to minister is to serve or meet a need. It seems to me that needs can best be met when one's attention is turned from the cares of the day to the message of the Lord. Music is an ideal vehicle for this.

There is also, however, a place for an artist to entertain an audience and make them glad they came, to give them music they thoroughly enjoy and leave them uplifted and inspired. This type of artist believes in the value of music for its own sake and sees himself as a musician who happens to be a Christian, rather than as a minister who happens to be a musician.

On the other hand, there's obviously a place for those people who either preach or share a prophetic message through their music. These artists see music as a tool to bring audiences to repentance or to a better understanding of and closer relationship with God. They see themselves as ministers and may even give altar calls at their concerts.

The fact is that the body of Christ is big enough for both kinds of artists. First Corinthians 12 explains that the body of Christ has many members and that each member is crucial to the overall well-being and functioning of the body. This analogy argues strongly that the various types of music and musicians perform a needed function in Christ's body. We Christians must heed verse 22—"The eye cannot say to the hand, 'I have no need of thee' "—and be not merely tolerant but openly accepting of various musical callings. Each musical style has a place, each of us has a unique musical calling, and all of these styles and callings have their role in the body of Christ. Personal preference of a certain type of music does not and should not invalidate all the others.

In music ranging from reggae to gospel quartets to rock and heavy metal, Christians are expressing their faith. No style is more "Christian" or more anointed than another. It is therefore imperative that Christians be supportive of an artist whatever musical style that artist feels he's supposed to use. We don't have to like the style, but we must carefully avoid judging the music or the artist performing it. Judgment is Someone else's job. Our job is to pray for and love all artists.

CHAPTER THREE

Getting Started As A Songwriter

Part I: A Basic Formula For Songwriters

If there were a simple formula for writing good, successful songs, I don't think anyone would do anything but write songs. That deeply satisfying feeling of finishing a good song has to be one of the most rewarding experiences a human being can have. Unfortunately, there is no formula for writing a "great" song because, basically, there are countless ideas about what makes a song good. (What appeals to one person may not appeal to another.) There are also various approaches to writing a song.

Very often, for instance, I am asked, "Which comes first—the words or the music?" As you write more and more songs, you will probably realize that songs come at a variety of times and in as many different ways as the thoughts in our heads do.

I usually enjoy blocking out some chords first and then coming up with the melody. I then record this rough idea on a cassette and drive around in my car singing fake words to the melody until some words come out which sound like a good title or which suggest an idea for the lyrics. When I am driving my car, I seem to be concentrating on the road so much that my subconscious has much better ideas than my

11

conscious mind. This may sound like a strange way to write a song, but it works for me. Whatever *your* approach might be, I can suggest a certain structure that will help you give life and order to your lyrical ideas.

The most common structure consists of the verse (of which there are usually two different lyrics to one melody section), the chorus, and the bridge. These sections most often appear in the following order: intro, verse, chorus, second verse, second chorus, bridge, and fade or last chorus.

The *intro* should be a four- or eight-bar piece of music (about 10 to 15 seconds) that has a taste of the chorus' melodic line. This is known as the hook of the song, and it is sometimes good to present the whole hook line in the intro. Other times, it is better to just hint at it so that the chorus has a greater impact on the listener.

Each *verse* should be no longer than 16 bars (about one minute) so that the hook in the chorus comes within the first 80 seconds of the song. Lyrically, the verse should set up the idea of the song so clearly that when the chorus comes you know exactly the thought being expressed. The verse should be the road that leads the listener to the gates which, when opened, reveal the chorus standing there in neon lights and explaining the idea you want to express.

Many times great choruses or hooks follow weak verses which have failed to prepare me for what was to come. When that happens, I'm left with the impression that the verse is one idea and the chorus another. It is very important that the song read as cohesively as any story you would tell or any idea you would discuss with someone. When the verse

12

gives clues about the idea or thought of the song which the chorus then clearly expresses, the chorus will make its greatest impact.

As I just suggested, the *chorus* should be a concentrated set of words which presents the idea of the song in the clearest, most concise way possible. In that 30 to 60 seconds—or 8 to 16 bars—you make your complete thought known. You cannot ramble or be vague.

The *hook* is the musical phrase with a melody line that is very easy to remember after just the first listen. It is the part of the song that most listeners like the most. If a song does not have a chorus that is easy to remember, it is unlikely that the words in the chorus will be remembered either. Since the primary purpose of a Christian song is to communicate biblical concepts, it is important for the chorus to be easy to remember so that the words in the chorus will also be remembered. The music in the chorus is like the container of a product: if the package is appealing, you want to see what is inside.

The *bridge* is a short section of a song usually between the second chorus and the start of a fade chorus. This is usually no more than 15 or 20 seconds (or 8 bars) long and is a different melody from that of the verse and the chorus. This is an ideal place to lyrically drive home or lock up the message of the song. It's also a nice musical break before the fade chorus begins. One thing that works well is to change keys and move up a fourth. Then, when you go back to the fade choruses, they will be modulated up a half or a whole step for the remainder of the song.

The *fade chorus* chorus is simply the same as the first two choruses except that it repeats over and over

13

until the volume of the song fades down at the end. Although this is not exactly the most creative way, it is probably the most popular way to end a song. Fade choruses could also lead up to a "cold" ending, especially if your song needs a "big finish."

As I have said, there is no definite pattern for writing songs, but a formula like the one I have outlined can make songwriting easier, especially if you're just beginning.

Part II: Getting Your Songs to the Right People

While there are many ways to get your songs to people who can help you get them recorded, here are some tips that may help you eliminate barriers and avoid wasting time.

• First, it is a great misconception that a producer or artist has to hear a completely produced demo of the tune in order to consider it for future projects. Although a well-produced demonstration recording is nice, most good producers can determine a song's merit with as little as a melody sung to a basic piano or guitar accompaniment. In many cases, in fact, a piano/voice demo can actually be better because it leaves room for the producer to imagine what could be done with the song. At times, a demo that is over-produced will not be as effective as a simple piano/guitar/voice recording in which the melody and words are easily heard.

A simple cassette recorder is therefore sufficient for a demo, but be sure that the lyrics can be heard above the music. It is impossible to evaluate a song when the words are unintelligible. A lot of instruments are

14

not as important as a clearly reproduced vocal. On the other hand, there are songs where the "groove" or production you hear in your head is vital in relaying what you hear to the producer. In those cases when production *is* a large part of the song (i.e., if instead of a lot of lyrics the melody is repeated by different instruments which come in and out and thus maintain interest), a more fully produced demo would be preferable. This kind of demo, however, normally requires a multi-track recorder, many musicians, and some studio expense. I suggest this route only if, first, you know of a relatively inexpensive studio and, second, you have friends who are musicians and are willing to help you out for a reasonable price. If you spend a lot of money on a demo, the chances of it paying off are poor unless it is good enough to be used as your own artist recording.

• Once you've made your demo cassette, mail it to a producer, artist, publishing company, or record company representative that records your type of songs. Keep in mind that a country gospel producer will have little use for a rock song and that a contemporary Christian song will rarely be used by a gospel quartet. After all the contemporary albums I have been involved in, I am still amazed at the number of quartet and country gospel tunes I receive from writers. It makes me wonder if they have any idea of the type of music I record and produce. The sad part is that, with a little homework, the writer could have sent the tape to someone else who might have been able to use their songs. A little homework is actually very important.

• Another important thing to remember is that most producers, artists, and publishers are looking

15

for original, unrecorded songs. There is not much anyone can do with your version of "El Shaddai." I received one tape on which a writer had put his Christian words to ten Neil Diamond melodies. Obviously (though perhaps not to that writer), these tunes could only be used with Neil Diamond's permission—which I doubt the writer obtained or even could obtain.

• Realize that there are as many different ways of getting a song cut as there are different types of food to eat. Four people—or even just one of the four—will decide what song is going to be recorded. Those four people are a record company A&R executive, a producer, an artist, or a publisher who might hear something in a song and convince the others of its potential. So if you've only given a song to one publisher or one artist, you've got one slim chance in four of your song actually being recorded.

If you have a publisher who's getting your song out and if you personally are also getting the song to artists, producers, and record companies, the chance of getting that song cut increases dramatically. Let me also suggest that you send the same song to all four people. One may hear something in the song the others might have missed. If you feel like Carman is the perfect artist to record your song, for instance, get a copy to him, to his producer, and to his record company. Have your publisher do the same—even if you have to send eight cassettes of the same song. In my opinion, such educated, thoughtful song plugging is much more effective than a random, shotgun approach.

• At this point, you may be wondering, "How can I get them to listen to *my* tape when they have so

16

many to listen to?" First of all, if you have established a relationship with a person, you can pretty much count on that person listening to your demo. On the other hand, if you don't know the person, don't send a long resume and bio with such details as what role you played in your sixth-grade play. Simply provide information that pertains to you as a songwriter or artist. Always send a photo of yourself to help the recipient connect a face with the song. A photo is especially important if you don't know the person.

Also, always send a new cassette. A tape that looks like it's had 20 other albums taped on it or one that has several layers of labels on the front gives the impression that the person didn't believe in his song enough to go out and spend two bucks for its presentation. I like to compare the presentation of a song to the effort to look neat and well-dressed for a job interview. In both cases, you're selling yourself. Let me just add that very few great songs have come to me on messy, low-quality cassettes. The great songs I've heard have usually been on brand new cassettes.

Another thing. If you can, find a colored cassette. A red, blue, or green cassette would definitely make your tape stand out. A red tape among a stack of black cassettes can't help but be intriguing. I know there's more of a chance that I'd grab that tape to see what it sounds like.

• Be sure to label the cassette itself with your name, address, and phone number. I've often had the frustrating experience of finding a cassette with a song I wanted to record many weeks or months after I have lost or thrown away the letter that accompanied it. At that point, there was no way to know who had written the song or how to get in touch with that person. It's wise, therefore, to always assume that the mailing package and the letter inside will be lost. Make sure that all the necessary information is on the cassette itself and always send a duplicate copy— *never* the original!—and don't expect the tape to be returned.

• A more direct way to get your songs heard is to contact an artist who is coming to your city for a concert. Concert promoters or local Christian radio stations may be able to help you. Most artists I know —myself included—are more than willing to receive a tape before or after a concert. Since they'll listen to the tape later, it's good to give the artist a picture along with the tape. Later, that picture will really help the artist remember whose tape he or she is listening to.

One avenue to the artist that is usually available is the disc jockey at your local Christian radio station. Since many artists meet radio personalities when they come to town, your local DJ may have some contact with artists who might want to hear your songs. The DJs also run into the local record company sales representatives who have contact not only with their home office but also with various artists from time to time. In fact, both radio personalities and sales reps have been very instrumental in helping me find writers and artists from all over the country.

• Last—and probably best—if you know someone who personally knows a producer, artist, publisher, or record company executive, ask that person if he or she would send to that friend your tape and a short note describing your talent and ministry. It's always preferable to be introduced by a mutual friend than to introduce yourself.

If you've done all of the above—if you've made several people aware of your tunes—and you have to keep reminding them of your song to the point that you feel like you are becoming a pest, chances are that your song is not what the artist is looking for. If you are turned down by every single person you play the song for, you could—and maybe should—conclude that the song still needs some work or that it's time to shelve that one and work on another. To complicate the issue, let me add that some songs that have been turned down many times eventually do find the perfect situation and become very successful. You have to make the call as to when a song should be put on the shelf.

Artists themselves have also had to deal with the application/rejection/application cycle. The band WhiteHeart, for instance, was turned down by every major label before they were finally signed by Home Sweet Home, and Rick Riso was pretty much ignored by everyone for six or seven years. I'm sure there are other examples, but the point is that you should never give up if you believe the Lord has given you tunes that really need to be heard. It's also important that you believe in yourself.

Let me offer some suggestions based on my own experience. On occasion, it takes some polite pestering to get a person to listen to your song and to take you seriously. I remember many cases where I finally listened to a tape because somebody had driven me crazy with phone calls. While all those calls bugged me, I did say to myself after one call, "I'm going to listen to that tape so that the next time this guy calls, I won't have to say one more time that I haven't listened to it."

If I listened to the tape and felt that it was weak or simply not something I could use, I just told the writer that I couldn't use the song. If I listened to the tape and heard something great, all of the writer's bugging paid off—and my earlier annoyance totally disappeared.

• One concern among writers is whether or not they need to copyright their songs before they send a tape to someone. In the more than ten years that I have been listening to Christian songs, I don't know of a single case in which an artist or writer has intentionally taken someone else's song and called it his own. Because there are so many notes and so many words, though, somewhere down the line you may hear a song that sounds similar to yours, but even in that case, I would say the chances are slim that anyone intentionally took your song.

That point aside, if you still want to protect your song, an informal but effective way to do so is to send a cassette copy of the song to yourself. When the package arrives, don't open it. Instead, put it in a safe place. By doing this, you will have a postmarked, sealed envelope with your song in it in case there is ever a question about when you wrote the song.

A formal copyright of each song could cost as much as $25 per song, the approximate cost of filing for the copyright and having the lead sheet made. To obtain the necessary forms and instructions, request circular PA from the Register of Copyrights, Library of Congress (Washington, D.C. 20559).

I hope that the last few pages have suggested a plan by which you can get your songs heard by the right people. Don't defeat yourself at the beginning with the thought that nobody will want to hear your songs.

20

Those of us who look for songs want to find a great song as much as the writer of that great song wants it to be found. Believe in your songs, and make a genuine effort to get them heard.

Part III: Getting Your Songs Published

When it comes to finding music publishers for your tunes, there are many points to consider. First of all, don't blindly sign with a publisher just because of its major name. Instead, think about the kinds of songs you write and then look at the kinds of songs which that publisher has had the most success getting recorded. Choose three publishers that might be good for you and set up a meeting with each one. After the meetings, you will be able to decide which publisher you feel best about and which one seems to share your vision for your songs.

The best way to arrange a meeting is to first send a tape of the three or four songs which most accurately represent your style and then follow that up with a phone call. (See the previous section for tips on submitting demos.) If, when you call, the publisher hasn't listened to your tape yet, call back. Keep calling back until they say, "Yes, I've heard it." They should also give you some type of response like "It's great," "It's bad," "We have no use for it," whatever. If the response is at all positive, ask if you could set up a meeting. By the way, I recommend using the telephone rather than writing letters. Letters are okay if you simply cannot get the person on the phone, but phone calls are a more personal contact—and they're harder to ignore. Furthermore, a letter calls for a letter in return, and many publishers don't have time to send much more than a standard form letter.

What happens if the publisher is interested in your song? Some new writers have the misconception that they make nothing else after selling their song. That's not true. The term "selling songs" is actually a misnomer. More accurately, the transaction between writer and publisher is the writer's decision to turn over the controlling rights of his tune to a publisher. That is, in fact, exactly what happens. When a publisher does buy a song outright—again, that is very rare—he may pay a writer in advance so they can create rather than work at the local Burger King. (Nothing against Burger King—it's just not a good place to write!) The publisher may also help the writer with an advance, but very seldom does a publisher say, "Here's a check for x number of dollars. Now I own this song and you'll never see anything else."

In the rare case when an outright purchase does happen, the writer must understand beyond a shadow of a doubt that he is selling *all* rights to the song. This fact needs to be spelled out very clearly. As I've explained, though, in most cases the writer basically transfers all rights and controlling interest in the song to the publisher. In exchange, the publisher will pay the writer roughly 50 percent of the income generated by the song except for the airplay income which is paid directly to the writer and the publisher by the performance organization such as ASCAP, BMI, or SESAC to which they are signed.

What does a publisher do for you once you've signed a song with him? First of all, the publisher "owns" the song. Also from that point on, he is forever obligated to pay the writer royalty income for the exploitation of the song as long as he owns it. Roughly half of the income will always remain with the writer.

For his half, the publisher does a tremendous amount of work for the songwriter. It is up to him to work with the writer as a sounding board during the writing of the song; to license it with ASCAP, BMI, or SESAC; to copyright it with the Library of Congress; to make a lead sheet of the tune; and license any recordings and other uses of the song.

Once the business arrangement has been made, it's up to the publisher to try to get the song recorded by whomever he can. This means pitching the song in as many places as possible. In general, good publishers are well-connected and very much aware of which artists need songs. Good publishers will usually be able to get your song heard in places you might find difficult to reach. Also, once a song is recorded, the publisher is responsible for getting other people to record (or "cover") the tune. The bigger a song is, the more important it becomes to get sheet music printed and to get it in as many songbook folios as possible. Finally, the publisher is obligated to pay the writer—twice a year, four times a year, whatever the contract says.

Another note on finding a publisher. No matter how great your song is, if it doesn't get to the right people and if it's not heard in the right circumstances, it's highly unlikely that you'll ever have anything done with your song.

In reading about the responsibilities of a publisher, you may have considered taking care of those matters yourself. You may have asked yourself at what point you should have your own publishing company rather than having another publishing company handle your songs. After all, by acting as your own publisher and keeping the 50 percent of the revenue the publishing company gets, you might be financially ahead of the game. Let me caution you here. If you're a new songwriter who doesn't know many people, it is imperative to have a publisher who is well-connected, well-known, and well-acquainted with everybody in the industry. Most successful publishers know almost everyone in the Christian music community and are able to contact almost any producer, artist, manager, or record label without too much difficulty. This kind of network comes only after years of developing relationships with those people.

Furthermore, signing with a publisher who is very successful in getting your tunes out to artists and producers allows you the freedom to write and create and do what writers do best. Writers write songs, and even great writers do not necessarily pitch tunes well. Besides, time spent pitching tunes is time that could have been used to write a song.

By the same token, however, a writer should never sign with a publishing company and then move to Alaska and just write songs, thinking it's not important for him to know anybody. No matter how good a publisher is, there's always a greater chance of a tune getting cut when both the writer and the publisher are constantly exploring different avenues which might lead to having it recorded.

"I get as many songs cut as my publisher does"— I've heard this said by writers many times. They may be right in some cases, but if they looked closely, they would probably find that their success was due to the contacts the publisher had introduced the writer to. A good publisher tends to open doors for a writer—doors to writing with other writers and to dealing with other publishers, producers, and record companies. Many times writers will forget that they have these relationships only because the publisher first opened the doors after the writer had signed with them. In my opinion, a writer should pitch his songs as much as possible, always being careful not to end up writing only ten percent of the time and pitching 90 percent of the time.

Should you decide to establish your own publishing company (or if you already have one), the primary purpose should be to be a publishing company. The motivation should not be to make a little more money off your own tunes. This motive can be "penny-wise and pound-foolish." While you may own 100 percent of your tune, you may not be able to do even one percent of what could be done if a publisher were working your tune. Financially you may not come out any better—and you could even do worse.

When a writer does decide to be his own publisher, it is crucial that he understands all the legal aspects, all the licensing aspects, and all the aspects of publishing overseas. With half of the record business happening overseas, the first question I ask a writer who wants to start his own publishing company is, "Who are your sub-publishers around the world going to be?" In my opinion, if the writer can't answer that question, he shouldn't be his own publisher. Music publishing is a more complex business than it looks, and someone who is unable to answer a basic question about sub-publishing should probably consider letting someone else publish their material.

In my opinion, a writer should have his own publishing company only if he truly understands publishing, and even so he should still probably hire someone to run it. If a writer understands the legal aspects of publishing, if he has good contacts, if he is knowledgeable enough to be able to get songs to whomever he wants, and if he realizes he will be responsible—for the life of the song—for paying the writer his due, then owning a publishing company is something that writer should consider.

Having considered working with an independent publishing company and owning your own, look now at a third option—those publishing companies which own a record label. Word Music owns Myrrh, Day-Spring, Canaan, and Word Records; Home Sweet Home Music and Bug and Bear Music own Home Sweet Home Records; and Star Song publishing company has Star Song Records. The list goes on, and it includes companies of various sizes.

Home Sweet Home Records, for example, puts out 10-12 albums a year. That means we have to find 100-120 songs per year to put on those albums. Practically speaking, we're not going to cut only tunes which we publish and we're not necessarily going to have 100-120 of our own tunes recorded. Still, with Home Sweet Home Records, a writer has immediate access to artists who are looking for songs for their albums as well as immediate access to the approximately 120 open slots for our albums. A writer with our company will not necessarily be favored over other writers, but our writers will definitely have all of their songs heard and seriously considered.

Word, on the other hand, puts out dozens of albums annually. Word Music has direct access to most of those albums, and their songs will be considered for the various recording projects. This kind of direct link to a record company is a good reason—but certainly not the only reason—to sign with a publishing company. The fact is that such a company gives its writers a tremendous chance to have their songs recorded. Of course, no writer will get on all the albums, but writers can be sure that a number of artists will listen to their songs and consider them very seriously.

I would recommend to a new writer a publishing company that is tied to a label. The company would give the writer an immediate base with its own in-house label and as much freedom outside as any independent company would allow. Outside of that in-house label, a new writer would approach all the other recording artists with as much of a chance of getting his/her songs heard as anyone else has. In my opinion, signing with a publishing company that is tied to a label offers the best of two worlds.

Let me close with a real-life example of a writer who has greatly benefited from an arrangement like this. When Dwight Liles started out, I was producing The New Gaither Vocal Band. Dwight happened to write "God and I Make a Majority," "He Came Down to My Level," and "Living Sacrifice." Those songs were recorded not solely because I was producing Bill Gaither or because Dwight Liles wrote them, but because Dwight is one of our writers and I was *aware* of his tunes. I played the songs for Bill Gaither who, as a publisher, had no financial interest in the tunes. But Bill loved the songs and felt they were perfect for that particular project. Once again, Dwight's songs were heard because Dwight was signed to a company connected with the project.

Despite the difficulty of getting a song to the right people, I believe that a great song cannot be hidden forever. A writer's songs can become successful at different times in the life of the song and in the life of the writer. On occasion, a song written way back will be discovered and made popular. Remember that the time is the Lord's when it comes to making the seeds we plant bear fruit. Realize, too, that while some writers find the right combination of producer, artist, and label immediately, others search for years. Still, it is my firm conviction that a great song will eventually have its day.

CHAPTER FOUR

Jeremy Dalton
On Songwriting

S ongwriting—men and women expressing their faith in Jesus Christ, sharing
their experiences and insights into God's Word, and,
perhaps most important, creating songs of praise—
is the most important aspect of Christian music. It
may come as a surprise to some of you that good
songs are in great demand among Christian recording
artists. Almost all the singers recording today use
some, if not all, outside material (that is, material
written for them by other songwriters). I personally
know of artists and producers who listen to a hundred
or more songs just to find ten they want to record.
This fact leads to the point of my contribution to this
book: how to make your song one of the ten.

Let me start by telling you a little about my own
personal experience in songwriting. I started writing
when I was around sixteen years old and, much to
my parents dismay, although I was a Christian, I wasn't
writing Christian songs. I spent quite a few years playing in bands and improving my songwriting skills until
I was in my early twenties. I had penned over 50
songs and still hadn't written a song about the
Lord when some very good friends of mine began
to pursue a career in Christian music. When they

asked me to write for them, I thought this would be an easy enough task, but much to my surprise, it wasn't. I had acquired plenty of songwriting skills and the music was not a problem, but I found that I really had nothing to say. I was trying to find clever ways to tell about the Lord, but the result seemed empty and not even that clever. So I began studying God's Word and listening to teaching tapes, and it wasn't long before I began finding all kinds of things to say. Soon I forgot that I was writing for my friends' album or, for that matter, anyone's album. I was just writing to express what was growing in my heart and, more important, I was writing to bring pleasure to the Lord.

The first of these offerings was a song called "Safe," which would many years later be recorded by Steve Archer and Marilyn McCoo. Then I began writing songs of praise for my church, The Gathering. At that time, I still wasn't thinking about my songs being recorded. I was just having a great time writing songs for the Lord. During this time, I wrote "I'll Do My Best," "Walk Like He Walks," "Oh Magnify the Lord," and "Everything I Am." My friends, meanwhile, had recorded a demo of "Safe" and were beginning to look for a record company. The tape fell "accidentally" into the hands of Chris Christian and eventually Bug and Bear Music with whom I signed a publishing agreement. We recorded "Through His Eyes of Love" with my good friend, Steve Archer, (Thanks, Steve!)—and the song went No. 1!

Now, after having nearly 20 songs recorded, I am continuing my endeavor to please just the Lord. Sometimes that's much harder than it sounds because there are pressures to fit into someone else's mold or to compromise musical and spiritual convictions.

I am not saying that you shouldn't tailor a song to another artist's sound. On the contrary, a good song-writer should be able to write in many different styles and still keep the focus on the ultimate goal. Let me offer the example of a song I wrote specifically for Dan Peek called "Doer of the Word." Musically, the song was influenced by the "America" sound that Dan helped to make famous, but it still expressed a valuable truth that I needed to constantly remind myself of.

Now, writing songs just to please the Lord should in no way be an excuse not to write quality songs. Writing for His pleasure should inspire us to work hard at improving our writing skills. Many times I hear inexperienced songwriters say, "The Lord gave me this song." Of course they think then that the song must be good—to which I have thought to myself, "Then why do all your songs only have the same three chords in them? Are those the only chords that the Lord knows?" Actually, I believe that the Lord gives us creativity and inspiration so that we can give Him songs. What we should say is, "The Lord *inspired* this song." Most of us start out writing songs with the few chords that we know. Then the Lord gives us a little extra creativity beyond our natural ability. It's just like an athlete who works hard to perfect his athletic ability. On the day of the race, the Lord will give him a little something extra to push him over the top. We songwriters must work hard to perfect our musical ability and then trust the Lord for the special inspiration we need to write great songs. Ideally, every time we finish a song, we should listen to it and be able to say, with some sense of wonder, "How did I do that?"

This may not be the practical advice you've been looking for. It's my firm belief, though, that if in your songwriting you endeavor to please the Lord first, in time you will find your songs very pleasing to Christian artists, producers, publishers, and others as well.

CHAPTER FIVE

Getting Started As An Artist

I f you feel that the Lord has called you to either a ministry or a career as an artist, you should first determine whether you are called to work on a local, regional, or national level. Once the scope has been established, you can take the following steps.

The most critical part of starting and sustaining a career as an artist involves finding or writing great songs which are musically appealing, which are lyrically moving or thought-provoking, and which convey their message in a fresh, creative way. These songs can be in a vast variety of styles—from a hooky pop musical format to a more mellow worship and praise song. Whatever the style, though, the songs must be the kind that people want to sing along with or hear again. In the pop music field, such a song would be called a "hit." For lack of a better term, I will use the word "hit" for a great Christian song, even though it doesn't necessarily fit the purpose of Christian songs.

If finding hit songs were easy, albums could be started and produced in half the time. Instead, finding or writing great songs is like looking for a toothpick in a haystack. Even so, it is the first and most important step toward becoming an artist. While many wonderful singers love the Lord, the ones who have the best chance of being heard are those who sing new or original "hit" Christian songs. I receive many tapes from people with a good voice who are singing their own version of "Praise the Lord" or "El Shaddai." No matter how dedicated that artist may be, there's little anyone can do for a new artist whose only songs are those that have already become well-known. Think about it. A radio station would probably play the original hit and a listener would probably buy—or listen to—the original version. Few, if any, radio stations or listeners would be interested in a new artist who released an old hit.

The challenge is to find something original. Again, the task is to find publishers who tend to publish the kinds of tunes that you are looking for. If you think you would like to sing songs like WhiteHeart's, find out who publishes WhiteHeart's tunes and contact the company. If you think you'd like to do songs like Carman's, look on one of his records to see who publishes his tunes. You can find out how to reach publishers by checking with the record company. Then call the publishers and tell them that you would like to review some of their tunes. Let them know what kind of music and lyrics you want. Part of a publisher's job is to review your request and to select a few tunes—out of their hundreds or thousands— which meet your needs.

The course of action I just outlined may take a little persistence, but nearly every publisher will send you some songs without charging you. Understandably, the publishers may not send you a song they've just sent to Sandi Patti or Amy Grant. On a more positive note, let me say that there are many tunes in our catalog that I know are hits—I just haven't been able to convince anybody else of that—and I'll send out those tunes. So don't expect to get every great song a publisher has, but, out of five tunes, you just might get one great song.

Why would publishers send out their songs free of charge? They do so in hopes that you'll record one of these songs and that somehow your recording will find its way onto an album. That's how the publishers and their writers earn their income.

An alternative to dealing with publishers is to go directly to songwriters. This approach to finding tunes is more difficult. It calls for *you* to decide the quality of a song whereas tunes you acquire from a publisher have already been screened and accepted by that publisher. Still, you *can* go directly to writers. Contact any local or regional writer you know. If you have a friend living in another city who knows of a writer, ask your friend to look for you. Contact anyone you know who writes Christian tunes, and listen to every song that you can. Out of all the songs you get, you may not find even one song that is right for you—but then again you just may find one or more great ones. Let me say that this process is very subjective. Even the best producers and artists pass up a great song from time to time.

Another difficult aspect of using local writers is that you almost have to be your own A&R person. You have to decide which tune, if recorded properly, will land you a record deal. The odds of a person new to the industry making the right decision are slim. Publishers who send you songs, however, are experienced at choosing songs for other people. For that reason—though not that reason alone—contacting publishers is a more effective way to go. Even if you don't get their best song, their "B" song is likely to be better than the songs you might find on your own.

It is not necessary, by the way, to send a tape of your voice to the publisher when you're looking for songs. A publisher is not necessarily going to be able to hear your voice and know what other songs you can or can't do. In fact, sending your tape to a publisher could actually be counterproductive. The tunes you sing might lock them into just pitching you songs similar to those on your tape. On the other hand, if you tell publishers that you want a certain type of lyric and a particular style of music, they may come up with something that you never would have thought of.

Once you've found the songs you want to record for your demo tape, you still face some options. You can, for instance, make a simple voice and piano or guitar recording on a cassette tape. (Make sure that the words can be understood!) You could also choose to go into a multi-track studio (cost and accessibility must be considered) and hire the best musicians you can to help record your demo. If this route would be too costly, start with a single cassette recording and get some feedback on the song first.

As you make more and more demo recordings, you'll notice your own growth and development. Therefore, spending too much on your very first recording may result in disappointment when you look back on it later. You may regret having spent so much time, effort, and money when—as you'll see later—you were so new and inexperienced at the time. As you continue to listen to other artists' records and compare them to your demos, you will come to know when it's time to make a fully produced demo.

No matter at what level you are, though, send your tapes to record producers, record companies, artists, and any contacts you have in Christian radio. (See the steps outlined in the previous chapter.) You never know which tape might find its way to someone who would be interested in you as an artist.

As your singing improves and your repertoire of good songs expands, contact a local church, a Christian bookstore owner, or a concert promoter and find out if there are any places in your area where you could sing. These appearances will give you valuable experience, a chance to try out your songs, and, more importantly, a place to share with others your testimony about how the Lord is working in your life.

If you are aiming at a regional or national ministry, try to front (or be the opening act for) a well-known artist who is coming to your town. Besides giving you a chance to share with the larger audience that a national artist may attract, this opportunity will also give you a chance to be seen by that artist and maybe even a chance to get to know those people working with the concert promoters and the artist. Festivals are also great places to perform because of the large audiences and the number of artists participating.

I'd also encourage you to take a trip once a year to Nashville, Los Angeles, or Waco, Texas (whichever is most practical) and get to know as many record company executives, publishers, producers, writers, etc. as you can. If you find one good contact in any of these cities, you'll find it much easier to meet other people involved in Christian music.

Another excellent way to make contacts is to attend "industry" gatherings like the Christian Artists' Seminar in Estes Park, Colorado. Held in late July, the Estes Park seminar is a fabulous place to go because almost every publisher, most record companies, and many artists are there in a comfortable and intimate setting. You can hardly attend the conference without running into—or at least walking past—almost everyone once. If you don't know people, you just might walk right past the president of the largest publishing company in Christian music without even knowing it. So do your homework before you go and know who it is you want to meet.

If you attend the seminar, your job will be to start asking questions and finding out who everybody is. Estes Park is not the best place to play your tunes or promote yourself, but it is a great place to meet people. Most of the business people go there to strengthen relationships with their colleagues as well as their relationship with the Lord. If you're too pushy in that relaxed setting, you can offend people rather than help yourself. These executives are wary of being approached and, in many cases, they stay in hotels off the grounds to avoid being bombarded by "hopefuls." Everyone is looking for the next "somebody," but Estes Park is not the place to try to promote yourself heavily.

If you do get to know someone to the point that they can associate a face with your name, it will be much easier to contact that person a couple of weeks after you get home. Follow up your Estes Park introduction with a phone call and, whenever possible, a meeting. While you are in the Rockies, learn as much as you can at the various seminars and begin to develop relationships with people involved in Christian music.

Another important "industry" event is Gospel Music Association Week, held each April in Nashville, Tennessee. (The annual Dove Award ceremonies are also held during this week.) While GMA Week is not nearly as casual as Estes Park and fewer artists attend, many business people do make the trip to Nashville and many of them are ready to make deals. Meeting people during GMA is a little more difficult than it is at Estes Park, but you're still likely to make good contacts.

You should also consider attending the annual convention of the Christian Booksellers Association. Held each July, this convention attracts every national record label and almost every publisher. Since each company has a booth or display, you can easily locate those companies you're interested in. Because companies go to CBA primarily to sell product to retailers, however, the convention may not be the place to pitch your songs or your talent. Still, it could be a good place to meet people and to arrange for future meetings.

Whether or not you are able to attend the events I've just mentioned, you still need to set up meetings with the A&R person at the various record companies. This means going to where they are, and that's usually Nashville, Dallas, Waco, or Los Angeles. Why Nashville, Dallas, Los Angeles, or Waco, Texas? The answer is that Word Records, the largest Christian record distributor, is located in Waco—right where Jarrell McCracken founded it in 1950. Also, probably 80 percent of all recordings take place either in

Nashville or Los Angeles, and I would guess that the majority of the songs we hear on the radio and on records are written in these two cities. Also, The Benson Company and The Sparrow Corporation, the next two largest Christian record companies, are located in Nashville and Los Angeles respectively. Star Song Records, which has Petra and Twila Paris, is based in Houston, Texas, and Home Sweet Home Records, which has WhiteHeart, Steve Archer, and yours truly, is headquartered in Dallas.

Obviously, merely going to one of these cities won't guarantee success. But just as a skier is most likely to improve in Colorado and an oilman has a better chance at success in Texas, a Christian artist will be closer to the decision-makers if he is in Nashville, Texas or Los Angeles. Of all the hard-to-answer questions and tentative answers about getting started in Christian music, the only advice I feel to be almost universally true is to move to—or to visit as frequently as possible—Nashville, Los Angeles, and Waco. When I left Abilene, Texas for Tennessee, I knew no one in Nashville. Without tremendous divine intervention, I doubt very seriously that things would have happened the same way had I stayed in Abilene.

I can't emphasize enough the value of a trip to one of these cities. Before you go, though, schedule meetings with various people. To find out who you need to meet with, contact a Christian radio station or Christian bookstore in your area and ask for the name and phone number of the record company salesperson for your region. When you make contact with him, ask him to help you set up meetings with record or publishing companies or to at least give you a letter of introduction. A letter like that can help open doors for you.

If for some reason you can't get through to anybody and you can't schedule meetings ahead of time, I still recommend that you head for Nashville or L.A. with your bags packed, your cassette in hand, and your guitar in tune. When you get to town, look up the addresses of the companies you want to visit and walk through their front door. If they can't see you right then, tell them you've just arrived from Hometown, U.S.A. and that you would like to make an appointment. Don't be presumptuous and expect everyone to stop in the middle of their tracks because you showed up. Give yourself a week or 10 days in town so that if someone can't see you in the next two or three days, you can wait a few days for an appointment. When I first went to Nashville, Tennessee, I didn't know one person. I literally walked from door to door. Ninety percent of the time I couldn't even get in the door. When I did get in the door, the people didn't even like my songs. In the Lord's timing and with some persistence on my part, this pattern of rejection finally did change.

Some advice about rejection: be prepared for it. If you aren't ready to face some rejection in the beginning, you might as well not even try because everyone faces rejection initially. You have to believe in yourself, and you have to feel so strongly that the Lord has a calling for you that you can deal with the initial rejection and move on. You may be very fortunate and find doors opening quickly and everything happening in a short period of time, but that is definitely the exception rather than the rule.

As you've read this chapter, you may have noticed the disturbing reality that, just like in the "real world," relationships and contacts are extremely important in Christian music. I would never discount the work of the Holy Spirit when the Lord is working His will, but relationships and contacts are the keys that open the doors of opportunity. Relationships and contacts alone will rarely get you a recording contract or one of your songs on a record, but they will almost always allow you a hearing by people who can help you. The Holy Spirit may lead you to the proper people, but maintaining good personal relationships with those people is your responsibility—and it's an important responsibility if you want a recording contract or if you want your songs heard. Obviously, the quality of your song and your voice and whether your voice or song is right for a given project will ultimately determine whether you end up with an album or get your song on a record.

CHAPTER SIX

Getting Started As A Backup Vocalist

I f your desire is to sing backup on Christian records and in live concerts, you need certain skills in addition to a good voice There are numerous ways to get your foot in the door, but first I'd like to touch on the skills that are necessary for a professional backup singer.

Backup singers have the same role in a studio setting that the musicians do. They both are there to deliver to the producer the particular sounds and parts that he's looking for to complement and blend with every other instrument. It is not the job of a background singer to be noticed. A background singer is to blend in and enhance the artist's performance and thereby the record itself. Background parts are not the time to try all your fancy licks and new ideas. In general, backup singing is more a job of fulfilling the desires of the producer and artist on a particular song.

In order to do his job well, a backup vocalist should have a quick ear. He should first be able to hear the part that the producer recommends and then be able to repeat it on tape. Good pitch is also critical because each time one of the, say, three background vocalists sings off pitch, the other two have to repeat their parts also. If all the backup vocalists have quick recall and good pitch, the parts take much less time to record properly.

Along with these vocal techniques, a good backup vocalist should be able to blend well with whomever else the producer hires to sing the backup vocals. A heavy vibrato, for instance, does not usually blend too well. If you sing with a great deal of vibrato, it would be good to practice singing without any vibrato.

Once you feel that you have sharpened your vocal skills, practice your rhythm and your ability to stay "in the pocket" rather than ahead or behind the beat. Most musicians and vocalists rush ahead of the beat during their first months in the studio. For some reason, it always feels like you are dragging behind the beat when actually you are right on it. In fact, it's not uncommon for a new vocalist to rush the parts to the point that they're almost in between the proper downbeat and the previous beat. This is one of the trickiest skills to master, and experience in the studio is about the only way to perfect your rhythm. When you hear yourself on tape singing ahead of the beat, it is much easier to correct yourself. You can learn how far behind the beat you must *apparently* sing if you are to be in the pocket.

Let me offer a sidelight here. In a live concert, it is usually helpful if the vocalist is slightly ahead of the beat. This pacing helps give the song energy. If all the parts were sung perfectly on the beat, the song could sound lifeless or programmed. By contrast, being too much on top of the beat in a studio takes away from the overall groove or feel of a song. Although I can't explain these differences between studio and concert singing, I know that they really do exist.

Once your vocal and rhythm skills are together, learn to read various kinds of charts. Some background parts are made up on the spot in collaboration with the other singers and the producer, but most parts are written out to some degree in some type of notation. The most explicit notation of vocal parts would involve writing each note exactly as it is to be performed by each singer.

Popular in Nashville and also very effective is the numbers system. The numbers system is great for musicians and vocalists alike because it only suggests the relative distance the next note should be from the preceding note. There is no set key, so the key or parts of a triad can be switched in an instant. There's no need to rewrite each note when changes are made.

If what I've just said is Greek to you, let me explain. Whatever key a song is in, the note that is the same as the key is considered number 1. If the song is in the key of C, then C is 1, D is 2, E is 3, and so forth up to B, which is 7. A symbol can be put to the upper right of the number to indicate a flat or a sharp. The proper rhythm notes can be marked underneath the number. As an example, a triplet on the D sharp note would look something like $\frac{2\sharp}{\sqcap}$

This numbers system allows much flexibility in changing parts and keys. It is also much quicker to write out. Since most vocal parts are changed once they're tried in the studio, the numbers system is used mainly as a starting point from which to work out the parts. If the vocal parts become very complicated, writing out each note is probably the surest way to go.

With studio time ticking away, it is important that, as a background vocalist, you are as quick and professional as possible. As I mentioned, if one of the two or three vocalists consistently sings offbeat or off-key, it affects the job of the other vocalists, the quality of the record, and the cost of the session. With this in mind, work on your reading skills, your tempo skills, and your pitch until you feel you are ready. At this point—and only at this point—would I recommend that you pursue making contacts and looking for sessions to sing on. If you work for someone before you're ready and don't do a great job, you may not be asked back even if later on you're much better. In summary, be willing to give yourself time to sharpen your skills. Be prepared when you start pursuing work.

Once you're in the studio, you face an area that is very subjective but I feel very important. The question is "When do I bring up my ideas? And when do I stay quiet and just sing the part I'm asked to sing?"

Obviously, the answer to this question varies depending on the situation and the producer. Determine for yourself if the producer has an exact part he's looking to have on the record or if he is searching through a number of ideas to find something that works. If the producer is still searching, I'd say feel free to make suggestions. Once you do, though, never try to win your point. Simply make it known.

I might also mention here that, with the clock running, this is not the time to joke or chat with the other vocalist(s). Most producer's respect a vocalist who has a professional attitude and is always attentive.

If, however, the producer has a particular idea and you can tell that he sees it isn't working, it might also be appropriate to make a suggestion. In general, be sensitive and exercise discretion before making a suggestion. I would, however, caution you not to appoint yourself as the vocal producer unless you are specifically asked to take that role.

The arena of the live concert is a different and much more flexible situation for the backup vocalist. For one thing, you usually have weeks to learn the parts and then you repeat them each night. That's in sharp contrast to the very limited time schedule and pressure of the studio. In a live concert, you also have to think about how you look and move on stage whereas these things are not important in the studio. As I have mentioned, energy and excitement outweigh being in the pocket in a concert setting and you—along with the artist you are singing for—must decide where the balance is.

I have intentionally described the qualifications for the two basic types of background singers before mentioning how to get started. If you feel that you are qualified or could be with some practice, consider a few ideas about where you might begin getting experience and making contacts which might lead you to becoming a backup vocalist.

The church choir is obviously the easiest place to begin singing, and it's a good place to start. Gaining the necessary studio experience, though, means a different kind of practicing than you'll do with a choir. Let me suggest that you play the instrumental track of a song you know and sing a backup part to the song as you have another cassette player recording both the track and what you are singing. As you listen back to the tape you made, you will be able to hear the places you may have been off-pitch and offbeat.

I would also suggest that you contact local studios as well as local youth ministers. Try to learn of any custom albums being recorded in town that you might offer to sing on. Even if you aren't paid, you will gain experience and knowledge that will be valuable when a great opportunity does come along.

You might also check with advertising agencies in town and get the name and numbers of jingle companies in your area. Jingle companies create musical commercials for clients. By contacting these jingle production companies, you may find a way to gain valuable experience and maybe even a little income.

Last, I suggest that, if you can, you go to Los Angeles, Dallas (the largest jingle market in the U.S.), Nashville, Chicago (another large jingle market), or New York to try to contact other working vocalists. Ask if you could observe some of their sessions. Even just watching professionals at work will give you invaluable experience as well as a chance to begin meeting some of the producers who hire vocalists on a regular basis. Also keep in mind that many singers (Brown Bannister, Janie Fricke, Barry Manilow, myself, and many others) even got their start singing jingles.

As far as singing backup for an artist, I suggest that you get in touch with various people—people such as radio station DJs, promoters, artists, musicians that tour, etc.—who are somehow involved in concerts. Make whatever contact you can with artists who may be looking for vocalists.

Whatever his or her tour schedule, an artist needs to rehearse in one city. Knowing that most artists live in Nashville or Los Angeles, I suggest a trip to one of those cities to try to explore whatever contacts you

48

have. Try to make yourself known and available to these artists. If you feel that a trip to Nashville or Los Angeles is not possible for you, then pursue local artists or groups. Explore their need for vocalists in the future. And don't get discouraged if you don't find a position right away. Not that many Christian artists travel with a full band and group of backup vocalists. If, however, you feel it is your calling, the Lord will open the proper doors in His time.

CHAPTER SEVEN

Getting Started As A Producer

P roducer (pra· doos'·er) n. The person who does everything from coordinating the selection of songs, studio, engineer, musicians, and arrangements, to being a focal point of praise or complaint from the record company, artist, musicians, engineers, artist's manager, booking agent, etc. The producer is responsible for, in one word, everything.

It is difficult to outline the "how-to's" of becoming a producer. First, everyone reaches it in a different way under different circumstances. Second, the creative side cannot be taught. It is felt and perceived in one's mind and heart. It is the quality and commerciality of imagination that gives a producer the ability to deal with the various musical and business angles of production. Finally, as in every creative process, there has to be someone who calls the final shots. Many people may contribute much of their time, energy, and talent along the way, but it is the producer who must coordinate the good ideas, eliminate the bad ones, and come up with a cohesive record that fits the style and direction that the artist wants— or sometimes does not want, but needs. The ability to function in this capacity can't be taught in five simple steps.

The producer's primary focus at the start of a project is to help select the songs for the album. These songs can come from a vast number of sources such as the artist himself, tapes submitted in the mail, songs submitted or pitched by outside publishers, and other established writers, to name a few. It is the job of the producer not only to select great songs, but also to select those songs that the artist will be able to perform well. An artist with a limited vocal range, for example, should not attempt a song that spans two and a half octaves. Neither should a traditional singer attempt a very contemporary or a rock song even if the song itself is great. The same artist who will sound great performing a song that fits his or her style may not sound as great doing a song in which he or she can't comfortably reach all the notes.

Once the songs have been chosen, the next step is to pitch each song in the right key. All too often this step is taken too lightly and the song is cut in a key that doesn't reflect the full potential of the artist. I have found that the difference of only half a step can make a big difference in the vocal power an artist can give to a performance. There is usually one key that, after much experimentation, emerges as the perfect key for that particular song and that particular artist.

Even after the songs and the keys are selected, there are still many choices that must be made regarding the production of the songs. Who will be the engineer? Which brand of tape should be used? Which studio will the sessions be held in? Which musicians will you work with? And which good arrangers are available now? The producer must keep in mind the intended outcome of the project as he makes these key decisions.

Also at this point, the producer must be aware of the budget and strive to make creative musical choices within those financial parameters. If a producer is working with a low budget, he may use one set of musicians for the whole album and arrange to pay them a flat fee for the entire project. When a producer has a larger budget, though, he may be able to call in different musicians and assign the best musicians for each song. Guitar players, for instance, who are great at rock guitar sounds and licks and not very good at traditional songs should be used on rock cuts and not necessarily on the whole album. Likewise, the rhythm players who may be good on the acoustic guitar and not so hot on the electric should be kept on the acoustic guitar.

Keep in mind that this same principle applies to vocalist, engineers and arrangers as you try to decide whether to use one for the entire project or different ones for different songs. Let me suggest, however, that using the same engineer will help insure a consistent sound and feel on the album.

One of the most difficult aspects of a producer's job is to keep all of the involved parties satisfied. The producer's two main employers, the artist and the record company, don't always share the same viewpoint. The artist expects the producer to be as creative and as concerned about quality as possible. The producer, however, is equally responsible to the record company that is paying the bills, and they want him to be as frugal as possible. Often the artist will want to spend a little extra on additional string players or another couple of mixes. The record company, though, may prefer fewer string players and only one mix per song. It's very difficult to be in the middle of these discussions, but it is the producer's job to arrange a creatively pleasing and financially sound compromise that pleases both artist and company.

Once both the artist and the record company are pleased with the mixes, the producer should then be present when the album is mastered. At this last creative step, certain parts of the mix can be altered slightly. Specifically, adding or taking away a certain amount of treble or bass in different ranges of the audio spectrum will give an apparent boost or cut on a voice or instrument. Each voice and instrument has a certain range that affects it more than others, and that can be applied to the overall mix to bring out or cut that particular voice or instrument. In mastering, however, you can only add or subtract equalization (EQ) on the overall mix: boosting a certain range of EQ to boost the vocal boosts everything else in that same range.

Although in most cases the producer has the final word over the creative process and enjoys the freedom to use his ideas on many different records, this fun side of producing carries with it a great deal of responsibility. The producer is at the receiving end of a multitude of requests from all parties involved in the project. The artist, the record company, the musicians, the engineer, the arranger, the studio, the songwriter, and the publisher all look to the producer for just about everything from the way a song turns out to being paid on time to being a spiritual confidant. Making the record as he hears it hardly begins to describe the extent of a producer's responsibility. A producer's job is the delicate one of balancing the opinions and desires of various parties and, with the grace of God, coming out of the project with a smile.

You can begin on your own to develop your basic production skills in a few areas, though. You can, for instance, listen to as many records as possible with headphones and try to pick out every individual instrument. In other words, break down each part. Once you can do that, try to recognize the similar patterns that emerge on different records. (Notice that the bass guitar is almost always played with the kick drum or that a lead solo or "lick" is never played over a lead vocal but in between the lead vocal.) In addition, come up with your conclusion of what, on a particular record, seems to blend together into a full, pleasing wall of sound and try to pick out which instruments and sound make that blend.

There are many avenues to becoming a producer. I began by producing a custom album that was later heard by Word Records; Brown Bannister and Jack Joseph Puig were first successful engineers; and Dann Huff began as a session musician. You must decide which of these various paths seems right for you.

If you are not either an engineer or a great musician, I suggest that you locate the studio nearest you (see Studio Appendix) and arrange to watch the recording process. Learn as much as you can about such diverse things as the engineering, the record business, where music has been and where it may go, and even how to bite your tongue when you want to say something but shouldn't. (This last item is the hardest skill to learn, but it's the one which is used most often.) Look around. Many schools and studios will take on an apprentice. The Gold Mine, our studio in Brentwood, Tennessee, has had some apprentices who have gone on to become excellent engineers and producers. While being a producer is one of the most rewarding jobs in the music business, it's probably one of the hardest to get started in.

CHAPTER EIGHT

Getting Started As An Engineer

Engineering is one job that can be learned more by watching and asking questions than by reading a book. The engineer is the individual behind the control board who has the job of making sure that each instrument sounds the way the producer wants it to. He also has to make sure that each instrument is recorded at the right level on the meter and on the tape. During overdubs, the engineer must get the instruments or vocals on the tape properly and keep running the multi-track master tape back and forth for the producer until he gets the performance he is looking for—all the while making sure that that particular performance is not erased too often. (Ha!) Once all the parts are recorded and it's time to mix, it is the engineer's job to equalize each instrument, to add echo and any outboard effects, and to blend all the instruments on each track of the multi-track together onto the two-track master tape—all to the approval of the producer. This is usually a team effort of both the producer and engineer, although sometimes the producer leaves a good percentage—if not all—of the mixing to the engineer. The producer, however, must give his approval to the final mix.

The engineer is often used by the producer as a sounding board for decisions, and an engineer can be very influential if the producer respects the ear of the engineer. Both Brown Bannister and Jack Puig deserve a great deal of credit for my albums because of the vast input they both gave during the recording and mixing of many of my productions.

Also, a conscientious engineer follows the mixes all the way to the mastering lab and is interested in hearing, if possible, the test pressing. (While the engineer is not usually paid for this final step, it is good for his relationship with the artist and producer—and thus it is good for his career in the long run—to follow the record through these stages.) Wonderful mixes can be greatly enhanced or greatly harmed at the mastering lab. Only a few people will hear the master tape. Most will hear only the record or cassette, not the 24-track. A project will be evaluated by critics, both professional and private, by how the *record* alone sounds. Thus, the mastering— the last step in the creative process—is crucial to the overall impact of the final product. Since mastering can harm a mix or make a master tape sound much better, it is important to use the best mastering facility and the most talented engineer possible.

What follows are some more steps to take to learn to be an engineer:

1. Try to hang around studios with the eye of a would-be engineer. Look for a paying or non-paying job as an apprentice or go-fer or anything else that might be available.
2. Take any classes on engineering that are available to you. Belmont College in Nashville, Tennessee has an excellent course on engineering.

58

3. Sit behind the control board at a live concert or, better yet, at a sound check that afternoon to watch how the engineer gets each instrument's sound and volume level and to see how he blends them all together.
4. Listen to different records you like back-to-back and compare their overall sound. Consider the different approaches that were taken in the mixes. There's no better place to learn than a hit record.

CHAPTER NINE

Getting Started As A Member Of A Touring Group

M any large Christian groups that tour year after year have been a great training ground for many of today's artists. It is also a wonderful experience for people who just want to know what traveling and singing for the Lord is like. These groups usually do not pay anything, and some even require each member to have sponsors. Still, they are great platforms for singers to use their musical talents and personal contacts around the world for the Lord. Also, with most of these groups making one album each year to sell on tour, valuable studio experience is gained without the financial burden or pressure that solo albums entail.

Since each group has different requirements and qualifications for joining, I have compiled a list of a few of these groups. The information will help you get in touch with them if you are interested in finding out more about their particular organizations.

Truth
P.O. Box 9553
Mobile, AL 36691
(205) 633-3000.

Jon A. Stemkoski
Celebrant Singers
P.O. Box 1416
Visalia, CA 92377
(209) 627-4000

Al Streder
Continental Ministries
P.O. Box 1996
Thousand Oaks, CA 91360
(805) 499-4393

Heritage Singers
P.O. Box 1358
Placerville, CA 95667
(916) 622-9369

Re'Generation
P.O. Box 40772
Nashville, TN 37204
(615) 292-0971

CHAPTER TEN

Nathan East
On
Getting Started As A Bassist

T he important first step is how one has prepared himself spiritually. Have you accepted the Lord's will for you in any endeavor you choose to pursue? After sincerely praying and seeking divine guidance and a better understanding of God's call to you, you can then think about the instrument.

It is important that you own a bass guitar that is set up properly and that is in good condition at all times. "Set up" refers to the neck of the bass guitar (it should be straight), and the frets should be checked to see that they are not worn down (that's usually caused by round-wound strings). It is also advisable to have fresh strings on the bass guitar regularly. Be sure to have these new strings properly intonated and adjusted. This is important especially if you intend to use the bass in the recording studio where you would want to have optimum sound and minimal problems with string noise/rattle or fret buzz. The pick-ups are another very important part of your instrument.

If you are not satisfied with the sound of your instrument, it may be necessary to experiment with different pick-ups or with different instruments until you are happy with the sound you are obtaining.

An instrument that is set up properly and has a good feel and sound will only enhance your playing and inspire you to practice. And, of course, diligent practice is essential if you are serious about becoming a professional. There are many different ways to practice. You can, for instance, play along with some of your favorite records or spend time practicing scales, finger technique, or various other exercises. The more time you spend practicing, the more familiar you will become with your instrument.

Once you feel comfortable playing the bass, try to avail yourself of as many different musical situations as possible. This is helpful in building a frame of reference. Many churches will afford you the opportunity to participate musically. Get involved in as many different musical activities (choir, school bands, orchestra, etc.) as time will permit. My first recording job was a direct result of a referral that came from my participation in various musical activities in high school. It was an album: for The Patti Family Singers; one singer was the young Sandi Patti.

Use the talent that God has given you. Be willing to get involved, meet people with the same interests, ask questions, and find out how much hard work is required to achieve your goals. Most important, enjoy playing and let the Lord's will guide you.

Chris has just asked me to answer the hardest question in the music business: how to get started. Wow! I have ten pencils sharpened, but I don t know how to put it into words.

(Nathan East is one of L.A.'s top bass guitarists in both Christian and mainstream music.)

CHAPTER ELEVEN

Paul Leim
On
Getting Started As A Drummer

Regarding my personal experience, I am a firm believer in prayer and positive thinking. Not *wishful* thinking. Positive thinking.

I have known what I wanted to be since I was eight years old on a farm in Texas. I've never had one moment's doubt. I always had a goal I knew I could achieve.

I've always been a goal setter. One goal at a time, year after year, step after step. Each time you reach a new goal, have the next one ready. Some are harder to reach than others. Some are musical and some are personal; some are easy and some seem impossible.

Each goal has led me to new people and places. Some of the incredibly talented people I've worked with and the places and records I've played on have literally been a dream come true for me. I am truly amazed sometimes and very thankful. God has answered my prayers for help and guidance. But again, there never was a doubt where I was headed, though many times it took longer to take the next step than I thought it should have.

Be patient, work hard, and listen, listen, listen. Listen to every kind of player and music you can think of. You *must* build your knowledge of styles so that you have them to draw upon in any and all circumstances. Being a player limited to one style is a sure-fire way to work part-time in this business.

Good luck and God bless.

(Paul Leim has played on many hit records from Lionel Richie to Amy Grant.)

CHAPTER TWELVE

Dann Huff
On
Getting Started As A Guitarist

I t is difficult to pinpoint exactly how one becomes a studio musician because the process involved is different for every person. However, I can share a few areas of development that may point you in the right direction.

The first and what I consider the most important step is to listen to as much music as possible. Be open to all styles and really immerse yourself in each one. When I did this, I soon found a player of a particular style whom I looked up to, and I bought every album he had played on. I then learned every lick that he played. Sometimes this meant listening to one bar for a whole evening in order to grasp the notes and learn how to play them. At other times, I just transferred the album to a tape machine and slowed it down to half-speed. More important than learning the licks, though, I was starting to understand what the best players were playing in certain musical situations. Later on when I was in a situation that demanded a specific part, I connected what I had learned from listening to other players with my own ideas and emotions and soon a part was born. Producers want musicians with great ideas, and unless you are a prodigy, it is important to draw from all the ideas available.

The second step is articulation. Learn to play accurately as well as aggressively. No producer wants a player who cannot play a part convincingly. He is trying to sell records, and in order for that to happen, he needs players who capture his vision for the music. Here again, listening to great players will sonically define what good articulation is. It is also important for you to hear yourself on tape so that you can compare the way you sound with the sounds of the best players.

The third and often overlooked area of development is sound. When I started playing, I worked on everything except my sound. It's worth noting, though, that ten years ago sound was not as crucial as it is today. The high-tech sound of today's records, however, demands that a player have a great sound. The good news is that never before has there been such technology available to the musician. But, in order to get a good sound and get hired, you need the right equipment, and in order to get the right equipment, you must be hired. It is a vicious cycle. I suggest buying good used equipment and placing special pieces of gear on your priority list. Here are my suggestions of top priority and then secondary equipment:

Primary:

1. A great sounding strat or strat-type guitar
2. An amp with good A/B switching
3. Digital delay
4. Chorus (stereo)

Secondary:

5. Compressor/limiter
6. Parametric E.Q.
7. Weird effects (cry-baby, blue box, etc.)

Be patient and remember that it is better to have a few terrific pieces of gear than a lot of noisy, cheap ones.

The last area of development involves your attitude. Remember that the recording business is a "people business." If you are a talented player with a lousy personality, no one will hire you. Also realize that this is a highly competitive field and difficult to break into. Your gain is going to be at the expense of someone else's failure to get the gig. So be gracious because there will always be somebody new and better. Usually, the more you improve as a player, the more humble you become because you realize that you will always have something in which to improve.

Listening, articulating, getting sounds, and having the right attitude all require hours and hours of practice and self-evaluation. Again, be patient. If you aren't, chances are that in your haste you will overlook many of the fine points or little steps necessary for developing your talents to the maximum.

(Dann Huff is one of the most sought-after studio guitar players in Los Angeles. He was an original member of Whiteheart and has played on several prestigious Christian and pop albums.)

CHAPTER THIRTEEN

John Schreiner
On
Getting Started As A Keyboardist

I n the high-tech world of contemporary music, the role of a keyboard player stands out as one of the most exciting and challenging parts to play. Today's keyboardist is being called upon not only to perform in concert and in the studio, but also to take part in pre-production and programming music into sequencers.

As a keyboard player wanting to progress in the music business, it is imperative that you take stock of your strengths and weaknesses in order to channel your talents in the most productive direction. This writer sees three fundamental prerequisites that an aspiring keyboard player should address.

Obviously, the most important requirement is proficiency at the keyboard, including a working knowledge of various styles from traditional pop ballads to frenetic new wave.

Second, one must be able to quickly and skillfully operate a wide variety of analog and digital synthesizers. Many times a producer will request a type of sound that he heard on the radio. It is your job to deliver that sound without wasting a good deal of studio time.

Last of all, it is very important to formulate long-range as well as short-term goals. If you want to tour with a band, you will probably acquire minimal studio experience. Likewise, if you want to establish yourself as a studio keyboardist, you could end up going long periods of time without work until you build up a good reputation. If your goal is to be active in the studio, then it is important to live where there are ample work opporrunities. Los Angeles and Nashville are currently the most active centers for recording.

Naturally, it is always difficult to get work unless you have experience. At the same time, though, it can be very difficult to gain that experience when no one will hire you. This writer suggests making yourself available for low-budget demonstration tapes. Work hard and then request a copy of the completed product. Besides giving you samples for prospective employers, this work will provide you with a wealth of experience. Above all, keep persevering. In the process, not only will you grow as a player, but also as a real musician who is able to meet the challenges that today's exciting music scene provides.

(John Schreiner is a studio keyboard player and producer living in the L.A. area.)

CHAPTER FOURTEEN

Jack Joseph Puig on Getting Started as an Engineer/Producer

I hesitated before I agreed to write something for Chris about how to become an engineer/producer. The only reason for my hesitation? I don't believe that a pat formula exists. Each person's entrance into the music business is surrounded by circumstances as unique as his or her personality. In light of this fact, I decided to begin by relating how I personally became an engineer and, later, a producer.

In 1972, I graduated from high school in the Los Angeles area and went on to college to get my Master's degree in education and then a teaching position. During these years, I was also very active in the First Baptist Church where I did the sound for the youth choir when it was on the road. In the middle of all this, I became more and more interested in engineering and recording.

Through a complicated network of friends, I met a man who ran a recording studio and asked him for a job. He insisted that he had no positions available in his studio and told me that it was extremely difficult to get into any aspect of the music field. While I listened to this man, I prayed that, if God really wanted me in the music industry, He would somehow

73

let me know *now*. Suddenly, God intervened. The man on the phone changed his mind completely. He told me to come to the studio on the following Monday and he'd find a place for me. At the same time, he said he didn't know why he was compelled to hire me. So, on the same day that I began my first job in a studio, I canceled my dorm room reservation at San Luis Obispo University.

In the beginning, my glamorous position in the music business consisted of mopping floors, moving equipment, and cleaning up around the studio. Basically, I was a "gofer," but in between the odd jobs I constantly kept my eyes and ears open. I tried to learn everything I could by watching everyone else record and engineer the different projects and by seeing how the different people worked together to create music. I continued at this studio for almost three years.

It wasn't until my job at a second studio that I was able to get any hands-on training as an engineer. This studio was smaller than the first, but there I was given the chance to apply what I had learned and the opportunity to grow and learn more. Every time I could, I stayed late and studied the console and tested the different sounds. I constantly asked questions of the engineers and soaked up every bit of information as if I were a sponge.

My whole life was learning to engineer. I wanted it more than anything else, and I believe that this is one important aspect of becoming an engineer/producer. You have to be highly motivated. You have to want to be a good engineer/producer more than you want to do anything else, regardless of the personal sacrifices involved in striving for that goal.

It is also essential to realize that you can learn from anyone, no matter what their position or status in the industry might be. You are never in a place where you can't learn from someone else. I was fortunate enough to understand and utilize this truth early on in my career, and I still live by it today.

After I had a few more years as an engineer behind me, I branched out on my own and became an independent engineer. I was fortunate to develop some friendships with people who believed in my potential and who taught me their craft. It took a long time—in fact, all of my time for many years—and I'm still realizing how much more I need to learn and grow. My mentor was Bill Schnee, and I will always be grateful to him for teaching me not only about engineering/producing but also about how to groom relationships as a Christian in the "Real" world.

Since going independent about five years ago, I have been blessed with more work and opportunities than I have had time for, but this is not the case for every engineer/producer. Certainly, the most important factors in any success I've had are God's grace and faithfulness. My relationship to Christ continues to be the dearest one in my life, and He is responsible for allowing me to get through the highs and lows of my career and personal life. Because Christ opened the door to my career, I will always try to give whatever skills I have to furthering the gospel through the Christian music that He led me to be involved in. I consider this to be a great privilege.

In light of my own experience, what follows is the best advice I can offer someone who wants to be an engineer/producer. First, make sure you are motivated. Don't give up and don't be discouraged if you hear "no" from someone. Consider whether you want this career more than you want anything else. Realize, too, the costs in terms of your time and energy as well as the costs that will be paid by your friends and family. If you aren't highly motivated, you won't make it. It's that simple. Second, prepare yourself for any opportunities that might come your way. Learn all you can, and don't be caught unprepared. Third, the music business is rarely all that it is thought to be. It is highly competitive, but I personally refuse to compete with anyone except myself. I've seen too many good relationships ruined because of envy and jealousy. These things are not of God and have no place in any career. There are some lovely fringe benefits in music, but it's a mistake to sit back and dream of these and of the glamour instead of preparing for a chance to perform and learn your craft. Finally, be prepared to humble yourself daily. Never think that you know it all. You don't—and you can't. In fact, realize that there are many other people out there willing to take direction and to take your place! When an opportunity does come your way, enjoy it. It's an exiting, rewarding career. When the music touches your heart and the hearts of others, there is nothing quite like it.

I hope that some of this will benefit you and that, whatever your career desires are, you see them come true.

(Jack-Joseph Puig is a sought-after recording engineer and producer living in Los Angeles. He has been engineer on albums for Amy Grant, Barbara Striesand, Supertramp, Steve Archer, and has produced such artists as Russ Taff.)

CHAPTER FIFTEEN

Making Your Own Custom Record

B ecause of the make-believe recording sessions on television and the relatively few recording studios around, most people have no concept of how a record is actually made. Most people would guess that everyone comes into the studio, that everyone plays and sings at once, that all of this goes down on the tape, and that—presto!—you have a record. Although this was the procedure until the '60s, it could not be farther from the truth today. The albums of the 80's are usually the result of more than 100 hours of painstaking overdubs and the product of thousands of dollars of equipment with the multitude of gadgets which make any instrument or voice sound different, if not decidedly better. What follows is an outline of the basic needs and fundamentals involved in recording a custom album.

A. Good Songs

Finding good songs is the least fun, most monotonous, least creative, most boring—you get the general idea—but most important step in making a great record. Most artists take the ten best songs readily at their disposal and spend the rest of their time trying to find the producer, engineer, studio, etc. and making the record. After producing or executive producing over 100 albums, I have learned that a rock can never sparkle like a diamond no matter how you polish it. By the same token, a diamond's sparkle cannot be hidden completely—even by a bad production or vocal. Either way, a truly good song is worth the time and energy invested in finding that tune.

Let me also say at this point that an average song is still an average song no matter how many bells and whistles you add. It can be made better, but not great. By the same token, bringing a great song to its full potential requires good production and great vocals. When this combination happens the result is a clean, perfectly shaped diamond we call a "hit." (See page 145 for information on finding good songs.)

B. A Financial Backer

Since each year it gets more expensive to make an album properly, the most important thing for someone starting out is to make an album that is neither under or over the quality you need.

You must, therefore, first determine what you want to accomplish with the recording project. Do you want to press a few thousand albums to sell at concerts locally, or do you want to make an album good enough to attract a major Christian record company and good enough to distribute nationally? Once you have set an objective, find someone interested in your ministry who may be able to raise the finances for you or perhaps invest in it personally. A local album can cost between $4,000 and $10,000 and a major label's album will be somewhere between $15,000 and $50,000—and even much more when the top musicians and studios are used.

Beware of spending too much money to be able to pay back your investor(s) yet not enough money to have a product that can really compete with major albums. Remember, too, that if you don't use the right producer, musicians, engineer, and studio, it will be hard to match the quality of a major album even if you have unlimited funds.

When developing your budget, you will find that mastering (preparing your tape to be pressed) and cutting parts will cost around $500-$1000. Also plan on a pressing cost of about a dollar per album once the "parts" have been cut from the master tape. This cost will, of course, vary depending on how many records you press initially. The more albums you press, the less the cost per album. You should be able to sell your albums at an equal or lower price than what your local bookstore sells its records—which, at this time, is somewhere between seven and ten dollars.

According to this formula, the investor will make about seven dollars per album, an amount which will need to pay for production costs, mechanicals for the publishers of the songs (five cents per song, 50 cents per album), and two to three percent of retail to the producer of the album. After the mechanicals and the producer royalties are paid, the total amount to apply against the album production cost is around $6.36. For the investor, this is a good return on each album sold, but the chance of healthy sales is drastically reduced if you don't have national distribution. If, however, you make a quality album and are able to find a major label who is interested, you might do one of three things.

1. Sell the album to the label at a mutually agreed upon amount and receive a royalty rate of around seven percent of retail, payable to you after the record company has recouped its investment.

2. Sell the album to a major label with no money up front but a larger percentage—such as 10 to 12 percent—paid from the first record sold until you are paid back your full investment. At the time that your investment is paid back, the percentage could drop to around nine percent.

3. Sometimes a compromise of the first two options can be reached.

If you feel that the Lord has for you a career in the music industry on the national level, I suggest that you make the best album possible. On the other hand, if you see yourself playing primarily on the local or regional level, I would suggest making an album of quality for the least amount of money possible.

C. A Producer

It is the producer's responsibility to gather information and provide an estimate of your total expenses. This list should include—for starters—payment for the producer, engineer, studio, musicians, copyist, tape, string players, and background vocalists. The producer will also review your choice of songs, offer objective opinions of them, and, if necessary, help you find other songs.

In my opinion, there are only two kinds of producers—good ones and bad ones. A good producer can cost between $2,000 and $7,500 as an advance that is recouped from three percent of retail sales (around 27 cents per album sold). A producer who is not the best you can get will surely cost less, but let me warn you that this is not the place to start cutting costs. Among the advantages of using a well-known producer is name recognition: radio stations notice a good producer's name on the list of credits and will almost always give that record a listen.

Another advantage is that his name is likely to open record company doors when it comes time to look for a distribution arrangement for your record. Review record jackets for producers whose work you like. They can usually be contacted through the record companies.

D. Beginning to Record the Tracks

Once the producer has booked the studio and hired all the musicians and other necessary people, it is time to begin recording the tracks. As a producer, I always ask the Lord—either with the artist or alone— to guide all decisions to His satisfaction and glory. Many times a song I thought would not be noticed turned out to be the one the Lord used the most. I try always to be sensitive to any leading of the Lord, even if it does not seem to be exactly where I envision a song or project to be going.

A lot of times a local group with its own musicians will wonder whether they should use them when making a record. After all, those musicians are familiar with the group, they understand the ministry, and they understand what the music is about. Or your group may wonder if they should hire session players that are the best even though they've never met them. A simple, black and white answer is this: Always use the best musicians you can find and afford. The fact that someone understands you, believes in your ministry, and has known you since you were three years old really has very little to do with the quality of the record that you cut. Even if musicians are good enough to go on the road with you, it is still, in my experience, much better to hire the best musicians you can find. Even though they don't know you, they can give you a record much

81

superior to that which you would make with less than superior players—no matter how well they know you personally.

Another question that often arises is whether all the musicians should be Christians. I can't answer that question for everyone, but I personally believe that the Lord uses many different events and people, directly or indirectly, to further His plan. I also feel that the quality of the album and the sincerity of the singer are the two most important aspects of any album. If the best musicians available for a particular instrument are Christians, this is a great plus because the spirit in the studio will be greatly enhanced by their presence and by your shared beliefs. But, in the final analysis, people who listen to the album will only be aware of the musical quality of the songs themselves and of the believability of the singer. Listeners will not be aware of the beliefs of the musicians, the studio owner, or the man who built the drum set. Furthermore, I would guess that only a small percentage of the musicians on major Christian albums are in fact Christians themselves. This fact does not seem to have hampered the outreach that Amy Grant, the Imperials, Russ Taff, and others have had through their albums.

It's also worth noting that many musicians who are not Christians and do not know the Lord have sensed the loving spirit of the artist, have heard the words of their songs, and, as a result of playing on the album, have come to know the Lord. While this does not always happen, when it does, there is no question that it was good to have the non-Christian players at the session.

Let me close by saying that I believe the Lord speaks directly to each of us. So be sensitive to His leading as you make decisions about studio players.

E. In the Studio

There are several studio tricks that can make your record better and help you gain some degree of objectivity in the mixing. If you know a lot of these tricks, you will also save a lot of time in the studio.

Tip #1: When you are ready to start cutting tracks, don't just hire any bass player, drummer, guitar player, and piano player. Instead, try to find musicians who will do the best job for you on each style of tune you are going to record. I wouldn't, for instance, hire a keyboard player who is used to playing "Amazing Grace" and "He Touched Me" for a Leslie Phillips-type tune. Also, I wouldn't use the same five or six musicians for the whole album. While some of those musicians might be very good for a few of the tunes, they may not be the best musicians for the other songs.

Once you have your musicians together, you should have charts written out that will give them a basic idea of the structure of the song. If you can't arrange for charts to be written, a simple demo tape that demonstrates your ideas and presents the flavor of the tune will greatly help your musicians know what the song sounds like in your head and therefore what you're looking for in the finished product. If you try to describe verbally what you're hearing in your head, there's a chance you may not be able to communicate clearly and successfully to the musicians. But with a little demo of your ideas, a session musician will be able to pick up on the flavor of the project and the approach you want to take even if your playing is not that good.

F. Beginning the Overdubs

Once the basic drums, bass, guitar, and keyboards have been laid down as the foundation, it's time to start layering in extra instruments and vocals one by one. These layers will help you achieve the emotions and sound that each song calls for. The order in which you add the layers is totally flexible. I usually like to put a quick rough or scratch vocal on the tape right away so that as I add other instruments or background vocals, I'll know the relative placement and level of the lead vocal in the final mix.

I would suggest that the musicians come in one at a time to overdub. Having a guitar player and a keyboard synthesizer player trying to do their overdubs at the same time could end up taking more time and costing you more. You could, for instance, need to let the synthesizer player stop and start over on the guitar player's best take. It's therefore very important to have one person at a time doing overdubs.

When most of the overdubs are done, I then begin to record the lead vocal. At that point, the singer can hear most of the parts and the instruments which will be on the finished record. It is my hope that hearing the track at this nearly complete stage will move them to give their best performance. It is much easier to sing with emotion when you hear an orchestra or a fully produced song as opposed to a four-piece rhythm section.

The amount of time one spends on overdubs has to be considered in light of the overall budget because studio time is expensive. Use the following guidelines for determining an average amount of time for each overdub:

• Guitar—one hour per song per guitar part. A double, or stacking, of a guitar part shouldn't take more than 15 minutes because the player simply repeats—or matches—the parts he has already created and played.

• Keyboards—two to three hours per song depending on how many synthesizers and piano overdubs need to be done. With the development of MIDI to link several different sounds or keyboards to one keyboard, much keyboard doubling or stacking can be eliminated.

• Background Vocals—one to two hours per song depending on the skill of the singers and the complexity of the parts.

• Strings—45 minutes per song if the arrangement has already been written out and requires few, if any, changes once it's heard with the track. Doubling or tripling each part usually improves the string sound if tracks are available.

• Horns—45 minutes per song if the arrangement has already been written out.

• Percussion—35 minutes per song. This is usually the last overdub to be done, but in most cases it is essential in giving the record a polished, finished sound.

• Lead Vocals—between one and five hours depending on the quality of the singer's voice and the mood he/she is in. It is ironic, but the lead vocal—especially on low-budget albums—is usually the last thing to be recorded and is often given less attention than the instrument overdubs. This is unfortunate because no matter how great the production is, the vocal will either bring the song to its fullest potential or bring the track down to a lower level. I can't emphasize enough that the quality of a song and a production is usually determined by the quality or believability of the lead vocal. In fact, a great production around a weak lead vocal functions as little more than a Band-Aid. A great vocal, however, can overcome many flaws in the production. It's for this reason that I recommend not cutting corners when it comes to recording your vocal. I would even suggest that you come in on another day if you can't seem to get your best performance on a particular day.

When you're recording the lead vocal, you'll ideally have 16 or 24 tracks to work with. You should also get about four or five vocal performances that you consider "keepers." Let me suggest here that you let the artist go all the way from the top of the song to the end. Sometimes when you start and stop, the artist loses the magic and momentum of the tune. For this reason, I ask artists I work with to go through the song as many times as it takes to get five vocals that I feel are very good all the way through.

All too often, producers fail to take the time necessary to get the best possible vocal out of an artist. They'll spend a lot of time on the guitar work, the synthesizer work, and the rest of the track, but when the artist comes in and sings the song two or three times, they think they have their vocal. In most cases, however, if a producer takes the first one or two passes as a keeper, he's not recording anything even close to the artist's potential. I would suggest that the artist continue to sing until the performances begin going downhill. This way, the producer can continually ping or transfer to the master vocal track anything that the artist improves on.

Once I have five keepers, I'm ready to do what we call "pinging": I'm ready to transfer those five vocals onto one track. If the artist sang the word "praise" better on track one, for instance, I use track one for that word. If the next word is "the" and he sings "the" better on track four, I use track four. (You can even work with parts of words and do such things as add an "s" on the end of a word.) I combine these five different passes into one composite, master vocal which is the best of each word or syllable. You are more likely to use phrases or verses than individual words and syllables when combining takes, but it is possible to get pretty close to perfection.

Once you have pinged down the original five vocals, do five more passes all the way through and compare the master track with these new vocals. If any parts of the new ones are better, transfer them over to the master vocal. In the end, you'll have 10 or 11 of your best vocals all melted down on one track, a result which is a far better performance than the artist will ever achieve live for the rest of his/her life.

One sidelight here. I've heard many comments about artists who don't sound as good live as they do on their records. When you consider that most recorded vocals are the combined result of between 6 and 15 complete takes under ideal conditions, it's not surprising that an album cut is far superior than any one vocal sung straight through will ever be.

G. Mixing the Album

Once all the instruments and voices have been recorded on the multi-track tape, it is time to combine them in stereo on a two-track, quarter-inch or half-inch tape. Each song will be run from the master multi-track tape through the control board where each instrument and voice is individually equalized (treble and bass subtracted or added), echo is added, and other special effects are applied. A number of pieces of outboard equipment can make each instrument or voice sound minutely or even drastically different and, hopefully, better. Then, after all of the tracks have been individually adjusted to complement the whole picture, the stereo output of the board is fed to the two-track tape machine and a master tape is made. This stereo mix is known as the master mix.

At this point in your mixing, it's very hard to be objective about the record you're creating because you've probably lived with the project for two to six months. If you've ever listened to a song for three months, you probably got used to it and lost your initial excitement about the song. On the other hand, you may also have had the experience of not particularly liking a new song the first time you heard it, but after enough repetition, you found yourself eventually liking it a great deal. In both cases, you aren't listening critically, and that's what happens when you work so closely on an album. After you have become used to the sound of your song, you are less objective than you were initially. As you're working on the mix, therefore, keep in mind that radio programmers and the public will make their evaluations after hearing the song only once or twice. For that reason, it is very important that the objective of mixing an album be to create a sound that will be accepted immediately upon the first listen. You definitely don't want a record that you have to listen to a number of times before you begin to enjoy it. This fact is especially true if you are a "custom" artist without a major label behind you. It will be hard enough to get airplay even if the program director likes the song the first time he hears it; getting airplay will be nearly impossible if the programmer needs several listenings to get used to your song.

How can you distance yourself from a project you're so close to? How can you regain some degree of objectivity? Let me suggest what Brown Bannister and I have done. After we got a mix we thought was good, we would get away from the studio atmosphere. I had a little car with a removable top. With the top off the car, we'd drive through the country around Brentwood, Tennessee. The horses and cows and green hills—it was an atmosphere totally removed from the studio and the record business. We would sometimes drive around for an hour or two listening to the mix as if we were hearing it on the radio for the first time. Somehow, when the song is playing at a low volume while you're driving in your car, you can tell more accurately whether or not the mix works. Somehow that setting allows for greater objectivity.

Realize that no record will ever sound as good as it does in the studio with the powerful amplifiers, tremendous speakers, and extremely accurate tape machines. But since few will ever listen to your recording in that studio setting, it is important that you listen to the mix on your own cassette player. Also, it is good to listen to a mix on as many different speakers as possible because a mix can sound dramatically different on different systems. In these real-life settings, you might hear something that needs to be changed. Perhaps you can't hear enough of the lead vocal, or maybe the guitar or snare drum is too loud and needs to be brought down.

This exercise of listening—and again I recommend listening in your car or on an inexpensive cassette player—is well worth the extra 15 or 20 minutes it requires. If after you've listened you still feel it's exactly what you want, you probably have a good mix. If, however, you hear some things that need to be changed, your mix is already set up in the studio and you can immediately go back in and make the minor adjustments. You'll probably have a much better mix in the end.

When all ten or so songs have been mixed, it's time to put them in the sequence that makes the most sense. Take into consideration the overall mood of the album, what you want to say, and how to keep your listener's attention. The first two songs on each side, especially side A, are most important because listeners tend to listen to those songs and decide if they want to hear the rest of the album.

It is also important to put the right amount of air between the songs. This step has to be done "by feel": there is no rule of thumb that will apply to all segues on all albums. It is just as important not to enter the next song too soon and break the mood set by the previous song as it is not to wait so long that the listener thinks that the side is over.

Most people think that the creative process is over once the album has been mixed, but that is not always the case. Once the master quarter-inch tape is recorded, listen to it carefully. Is there a part in the song that you do not want to keep? Is there a section that would be more effective in a different place? At this point, with a sharp razor blade and a sharp mind, you can take out any section of the song and leave it out or replace it with another part of the song. You can also make a same-speed copy of a good chorus and replace the first chorus with a copy of the second so that the song's first two choruses are identical. This editing may be tricky for the beginner, but it's an extremely valuable tool for last minute changes you may want to make. If you are not experienced at editing, make a copy of the mix and try your skills on the copy before you touch the master. You could also use an engineer who is an experienced editor.

H. Mastering

Mastering is the final step in producing an album. At this stage, the finished, sequenced two-track master tape is transferred from tape to an acetate disc. The only creative work possible at this stage is changing the EQ, altering the speed of the record, or possibly adding compression to limit the sound level—or dynamic range—of the record. (Vinyl discs have a limited dynamic range and usually requires a certain amount of compression. The compact disc format, however, is not subject to this limitation.)

Next, the mastering engineer will make acetate reference discs one at a time that you can take home to check on a familiar turntable. If everything sounds acceptable, the mastering facility cuts the "parts." These "parts" are the mold for the "mothers" (the actual stampers of the albums) and are sent to the pressing plant.

I. Album Cover

The album cover is crucial to the packaging of a record. While some people believe that the artist and the songs are 99 percent of what catches the attention of the record buyer, the fact is that stores will give poor shelf space (or no space at all) to an album with a weak cover. The artist and the songs are indeed the most important ingredients, but a poor cover can keep the album from even being picked up by a consumer or displayed well at a record store. If a car handles great but looks ugly, some people won't buy that car based on its looks alone. The fact is, people do judge books—and cars and albums—by their covers.

On the whole, the buyer of contemporary Christian records seems to like a pleasant picture of the artist and medium to bright colors. Although the secular record buyer may not mind an illustration on the front, I believe that the artist's face on a cover is crucial in the world of Christian music. The Christian listener is concerned not only with what the artist is saying, but also with what he is like. Obviously you cannot represent everything about an artist's personality or walk with the Lord on an album cover, but you can at least offer the record buyer a sense of what the artist is like. There are no hard and fast rules for the cover, but it is important to convey that the artist is sincere about what he is saying and that there is a calm, joyful peace in his life.

Most album covers begin with a photo session of the artist during which several rolls of film are shot. At this point, it's good to already have a general idea of the title of the album and of the look of artwork on the front and back.

You want the photo to fit in with the overall design. When proofs of the pictures are developed, the artist, the record company, and the manager choose the picture that best conveys the mood and message of the album.

Once you have selected pictures for the front and, if you want, the back, talk to a graphic designer about how to best enclose or highlight the pictures. The graphic artist working on your cover design will usually complete several ideas (called "mock-ups" or "composites") from which you will select one.

The recording artist must also decide what credits he or she would like to include on the back of the album cover, the album sleeve, and the cassette liner (the names of the producer, engineer, studios, musicians, vocalists, photographer, designer, etc.). In addition, it is traditional to include additional credits or "special thanks" in the album design. These are usually for people whom the artist holds as instrumental in his or her ministry, career and the creation and production of the record.

Most recording artists feel it is important to include the lyrics of the songs recorded on the record on the album sleeve and/or the cassette liner. If this is to be done, it is necessary to obtain the permission from the publishers of the songs to print the song lyrics and to include the names of the writers and the legal copyright notice required by the publisher. You will find that publishers are usually willing to grant this permission and without the payment of any fee or royalty.

Once all of this information is gathered and verified, the graphic artist will design the front and back album cover, the album sleeve, and the cassette liner. The credits and lyrics will be typeset and reviewed by the designer, the artist and other persons involved in the design of the packaging for possible misspellings or "typos". The misspellings and typos are then corrected and the designer completes a proof of the camera-ready art for the recording artist's final overall approval. After the final approval, the art will go to the printer for the production of color film and the printing of the album jackets, album sleeves and the cassette liners.

The cost of the photography can run between $200 and $750. The design fee can range anywhere from $500 to $2,000. The typesetting can run $100 to $300, and the jackets themselves will cost $.50 to $.75 each, depending on the quantity printed.

Rhonda Jesson is one of the best graphics artists working on Christian album covers. She has a talent for designing a clean, attractive cover that is right for the Christian marketplace. I've asked her to answer the question, "How do I get started as a graphic designer for albums?"

CHAPTER SIXTEEN

Rhonda Jessan On Getting Started As A Graphic Designer

To become a graphic artist in the recording business, one needs a thorough education in graphic design/commercial art. These classes should prepare you to work with clients, printers, photographers and illustrators. You will learn how to take a project from concept to finished (printed) art. The projects you complete in school will provide your first portfolio pieces.

The next step is to make an appointment with the art director or creative director at a record company. Some companies have their own in-house art department, other companies hire only free-lance artists, and others have both. I would suggest working in an art department with other artists for at least two years. This is a very good way to get practical training and to learn from other artists who have more experience. From this point, you can better step out on your own and try free-lancing, working your own hours, being your own boss, etc. Sound good? It is!

CHAPTER SEVENTEEN

On The Radio

N ow that you've done the record, how do you get it played on the radio? As you are no doubt aware, only some songs get played on the radio. Most don't. So what does it take to get radio stations to play *your* songs?

Radio airplay in the Christian field has become a lot more competitive in the past five or six years. When I produced *Home Where I Belong* and Amy Grant's first album, there was very little contemporary Christian music. All you had to do was mail the record to the station and you got airplay—a lot of airplay.

In the last five or six years, though, there have been so many great Christian artists, so many great Christian songs, and so many quality records that airplay doesn't come as easily. Still, it's not nearly as competitive as the general or secular marketplace where artists have to hire independent promotion people, but airplay on Christian stations is certainly not automatic—even for good records and known artists.

How does a major record label try to get airplay for your song? They send a professional-looking, quality-sounding single to Christian stations. Sending a single instead of an album helps the station focus on one song off the album. If they send an album first instead of a single, each station is likely to play a different song—in which case you will diffuse your chances of having a hit off your album. Furthermore, if airplay is spread across several songs on your albums, you'll never achieve that concentrated airplay that gets your song on the charts. (We'll discuss more about how the charts work in the next chapter.) In the initial stages, it's very important to try for national exposure with just one tune. Later on, after you've released two or three singles from an album and you want the stations to have the album, they can play whatever else fits their marketplace.

As I've said, the first step is to send your single to each radio station, but especially to those who report to the charts. The major record companies have lists of all the music-oriented Christian stations. With a little polite begging, you may be able to get a copy of their list. National Religious Broadcasters publishes a directory of stations as well. Write NRB, CN 1926, Morristown, NJ, 07960 for information.

After the single has been mailed and the stations have had it for about a week, begin calling them. Make sure that they recieved it and find out if they've listened to it. This first promotion call shouldn't be any type of heavy sales pitch. You should simply remind the program director or music director that the record is there and request that they listen to it whenever they get a free moment.

A week or two after you've made this initial contact, call again. At that point, ask about the station's plans for the record. In the Christian market today, the mere fact that you're calling and reminding them about the record may be as much promotion as you need.

Furthermore, a strong-armed approach to promotion would be improper because each station has the ministry needs of its region or its local city at heart. Songs perfect for L.A. may not be good for Abilene, Texas. The mere fact that you are interested enough to call the station two, three, or four times about one record lets them know that you're behind the song and that you'll do whatever you can to help support them.

As you or your representative does this phoning, let the stations know that you'll be glad to send, free of charge, singles or albums for them to give away on the air. Not only does this allow the station to give some free records to their listeners (which helps the station), it also gives you a great deal of free exposure for your record. With these kinds of promotions, everyone wins for a minimal financial investment on your part. In other cases, you might offer to have the artist call the radio station to do an interview. Or there might be a time when you can offer to have your artist endorse a radio station's share-a-thon or fundraiser. This, too, may help your record get some airplay time.

In terms of the big sales picture, is airplay really important for the sale of Christian albums? While it is obviously crucial in the secular market, nobody really knows what impact Christian radio has on sales. One label recently let its entire airplay promotion department go because some of their records that didn't get airplay sold well and some of their records that got a lot of airplay did not sell. Without a clear connection between airplay and sales, they felt they could not justify the expense of a promotion department.

As the owner of a record company and as a producer, I feel that airplay is crucial and that it is probably the only immediate way to break a new artist or new album. Even with established artists, airplay is important in letting people know you have a new record out. Frankly, we've had records by well-known artists that have gone all the way to number two on the *MusicLine* airplay chart and yet, to date, have not sold very well. But I don't use that example to say that radio airplay is ineffective. Instead, that discrepancy seems to suggest that some other area in the career or ministry of that artist is not where it should be. Concert appearances, management, and the extent of their ministry or commitment are other factors which contribute to sales.

While one important plus is the sales generated by airplay, there are also some immediate benefits for song publishers. Each publishing company is affiliated with what is called a performance rights society (ASCAP, BMI, and SESAC). In turn, each writer must affiliate with the performance rights society of the publisher he or she is signed to. These societies survey the radio airplay and watch the radio charts for songs of their affiliated publishers which are aired by radio stations.

These societies are responsible for the "blanket" licensing of the performance rights of the songs from their affiliated publishers to the radio stations, and the collection of license fees on behalf of the publishers and writers. They continually monitor the radio airplay and watch the radio charts for the broadcast performance of the songs on radio stations. When they pick up airplay on a song, they use a rather complicated system of formulas to determine the royalty payments that the publishers and writers are entitled to.

One more word about the cold reality of getting a station to play your song. Airplay for a "custom" label or independent project is difficult to get. Of course, if the record is exceptional, there's a chance, but the chance is not nearly as good as it would be for a song by a well-known artist that comes to the station from one of the major labels. When stations get a record from one of these established labels, they know that the record is also going to be in the store, and that by playing the song they'll by helping to generate sales for their local bookstore—a potential, if not established, advertiser.

If a station receives a custom record from someone in another town, they can't be sure that there is ever going to be an album in the local record store. If their listeners can't go out and purchase the product, there is less incentive to play it. There are too many other quality albums to play which *are* in the bookstores. Consequently, when radio stations have a choice between playing a major record release that is as good as a custom release, they normally go with the major record release.

Let me end with some encouragement. While it is not as easy to get airplay for a custom label, it's not impossible. In fact, some program directors or music directors may hear something very special in the tune that you send. Even though there may not be records in the bookstore, he may feel that your song will minister to his audience and he'll play the song anyway. A custom label, therefore, should never fail to send singles just because the odds are against them.

Remember that old adage: "If you aim at nothing, you're sure to hit it."

Another interesting thing that happens once in a while is that airplay will lead to an album getting picked up by a major label. If you can get the right stations to play your song, it's possible that a ground-swell "buzz" will get started. This can attract the attention of an A&R director who has previously ignored you and may open up the distribution network of a major label. (It is worthwhile to note that success will always attract the attention of an A&R director!) Whatever the odds, it is worth the time and money to service the radio stations if you believe in your product.

CHAPTER EIGHTEEN

The Charts

J ust like people in the general music business, Christian music people pay attention to the "charts"—to the tabulation of national sales and radio airplay figures. Radio programmers look at airplay statistics to see what songs are the most popular across the nation. Retailers study album sales charts to determine which records their store should stock. Song publishers, songwriters, artists, and record company executives look to this information as an indication of how well they are serving their public.

Is it important to have a single do well on a chart like the MusicLine 40? I believe that it's critical. While a chart position does not guarantee a certain amount of record sales, it really can help make the bookstores and public aware that your record is out. The bookstores are looking at charts to see which songs are hot around the nation. When they see a top five song or a top ten song, they are much more likely to order the album for their store. Needless to say, the more albums you have on display in the stores, the greater chance you have of selling them.

How does the charting process work? The publications which compile charts *(MusicLine, Billboard, Bookstore Journal, Singing News)* maintain a list of "chart reporters." These radio stations and retail outlets report their airplay or sales to the magazines. The publications tabulate the results using similar systems. Since *MusicLine* is the most popular trade magazine for Christian music, let's look at the system it uses.

For its top 50 "Album Sales" chart, *MusicLine* maintains a network of about 50 key stores from various parts of the country. It also utilizes the combined sales figures from major chains, making the total number of stores reporting more than 150. Since actual sales figures are used, determining the best sellers is relatively easy. The numbers are simply added up, and the album which sold the greatest number of units during the survey period will be in the number one position that month.

Compiling the airplay charts is a bit more complex. First of all, these charts are based on station formats and musical style, i.e., "Adult Contemporary" (MusicLine 40), "Rock," "Contemporary Hits," "Southern Gospel," and "Black Gospel." Again, the magazine maintains a network of key stations representing each format. The stations keep track of the songs they play during the four-week charting period and rank the songs according to how many times each was played. *MusicLine* takes these individual playlists and assigns the various songs points according to their position on the report. The top song receives 20 points; the number two song, 19.5 points; the number three song, 19 points; and so on. The song with the most points after all the station charts have been tallied will be in the number one position that month.

Since *MusicLine* and the other publications use the information from selected stations, it's critical that you find out which stations report. Only airplay on these stations will affect chart positions. Even if a song is getting heavy airplay across America, it won't make the chart if it's not being played by the chart reporters. This may seem unfair, but keep in mind that the chart reporters are carefully chosen according to their sphere of influence, listening audience, and musical format. If you're not being played on these stations, you've got some ground yet to cover.

Since the chart reporters are the key to getting on the charts, you may be wondering how to get hold of their call letters and addresses. While some of the magazines refuse to release the names of their chart reporters, *MusicLine* lists the call letters of their reporting stations below each chart except the sales chart. (They'll usually send you that list if you request it nicely.) Since only the call letters are listed, you may have to do a little research to get the addresses of the airplay reporters. (The addresses and phone numbers of many of the key stations are listed in the appendix.)

As you might expect, reporting stations receive a tremendous quantity of records and a great deal of attention from the record labels because it's very important to the labels that these particular stations play their songs. They are more than willing to give the stations almost any kind of assistance, whether in the form of records or promotions or special favors. They hope that this service improves the chances of having their songs played on the air and reported to the magazines.

As you approach radio stations with your songs, it is smart—not to mention cost effective—to mail records only to the appropriate reporting stations. If your song is a rock song, send it to the rock and CHR reporters as well as to the "MusicLine 40" stations. Obviously, you don't need to send a rock song to a Southern gospel station. Likewise, don't bother to send a Southern quartet record to the rock reporters.

When you or your promotion person calls the reporting stations to see if they have received the record and if they are playing it, ask the stations if they are reporting this airplay. That will do two things. First, it will remind the stations that they help you if they do report it. If they didn't report it for some reason but should have, they may include it on the next report. Second, the question reveals a knowledge of the business and an understanding of what is important for the label, for the radio station, and for the charts. Stations you have serviced with a single should receive follow-up phone calls from you, as we discussed earlier in "Making Your Own Custom Record."

As we discussed in the previous chapter, though, the real question is, "Can an independent or custom label really expect to get airplay?" In the case of the reporting stations, you'll encounter tight playlists and strict qualifications that a song must meet before it gets on the air. These stations receive a lot of calls, promotional pieces, and even pressure from the various record companies to get their songs on. You'll therefore find it much more difficult to get airplay on a reporting station the competition is much more intense than it is on the non-reporting stations. It's quite possible that many non-reporting stations don't even get records from some of the labels, so you may encounter less competition for airplay. While you are more likely to get your songs played on non-reporting stations, that airplay will not affect any charts which, in turn, eliminates one way of being noticed by a retailer who might stock your product. Still, airplay on any station is better than no airplay at all. Your music can still be ministering whether or not the station playing it is a chart reporter. But remember, an album that's collecting dust on a programmer's or retailer's shelf doesn't even have a chance of being heard by the right pair of ears.

CHAPTER NINETEEN

Retail

Getting your record in the stores is even more difficult than getting your song played on the radio. If you are on a custom label, the first thing to do is to try to get a major label to pick up your album. If you've tried every avenue you know and still haven't been successful, start with airplay. Send your single to all the Christian stations you can find. Watch all those stations closely. When you find that a certain station is playing one of your records, call the bookstores in that city. If you're getting airplay in Bangor, Maine, find out what Christian bookstores are located in Bangor and then call each store. Make them aware that their local Christian radio station is playing your song on the air and ask if they would be interested in taking five or ten records on consignment.

"Consignment" means that you will ship the records without obligation. If the store sells the records, it will pay you. If the records don't sell within a certain amount of time, the store can send them back to you. They pay for the postage but not for the albums. If, however, customers come into the store and request your album because they heard your song on the radio, the product is available. If the store sells out, the manager can call you back and order more records.

Obviously, it is difficult to follow the airplay of every Christian radio station in the nation and to call every Christian bookstore and send five or ten records to each one. It's much easier to sign with a major label that's already calling all the stores and all the stations, but if you can't get a deal with a major label, an independent distributor is an option.

While there are several distributors to contact, they generally function in the same way and they offer the same benefits to you, the artist. Working with an independent distributor means contact with the retailers and access to the mechanisms which will get your product to the stores. The distributor will also warehouse, ship, and invoice for you. Some even have sales reps on the road. (Spring Arbor in Michigan, however, only takes orders by phone.)

Working with an independent distributor, however, also means being one of thousands of records they are trying to get in the stores. You are competing with major artists on major labels in the ordering process, and it's very easy to be overlooked. Furthermore, distributors *distribute*: they don't generally create demand. That's up to you! (See the next chapter.)

When considering an independent distributor, be aware of their discount structure. If you deal directly with a bookstore, you will allow a 40-45 percent discount off the retail price. A distributor (wholesaler) will be looking for a discount in the neighborhood of 60-65 percent off the retail price. He will, of course, provide warehousing, billing, and fulfillment services for that extra discount, so this is less of a negative than it might seem. In fact, working with a distributor can be more profitable than trying to do everything yourself.

If, however, you cannot secure distribution through an established channel, self-distribution is still an option. And self-distribution can, in fact, be the first step for you. Word will get out about your album, and perhaps the news that it is selling reasonably well may reach the ears of a sales rep for one of the major labels. He could take that information back to the record company and spark some interest in your record.

As you can see, breaking into retail can be even more difficult than breaking into radio. The results can be worth the effort, though. I've said it all along, and it's worth saying again: If you believe in your calling and your product, don't let anything stand in your way.

CHAPTER TWENTY

Advertising, Promotion, and Public Relations

Have you ever wondered how a certain group got on the cover of *Contemporary Christian Magazine*? And what did that person do to get an interview in *Christian Life*? What about that great ad in *The Christian Reader*? How do you end up getting a full-page, four-color ad on the back cover of *Charisma*?

The answer to these questions is advertising, promotion, and public relations—fields which work toward the one goal of creating demand. And demand for your product must be inspired in both the trade and the consumer. "Trade," of course, refers to the industry itself. It stands to reason that you have to sell to the sellers before you can sell to the consumers. One of your first considerations, then, should be, "How can I create demand at the levels of radio, retail, and concert promotion?"

Several publications serve the Christian music trade. For retailers, there's *Bookstore Journal* and *Christian Bookseller*. These magazines are sent free of charge to every Christian bookstore in the U.S. These two magazines, however, offer very little coverage of Christian music. *Billboard* provides the best music coverage in the world, but they deal very little with

Christian music. Subscriptions are expensive, too. *The Singing News*, another all-music publication, is not all-trade: it primarily covers Southern gospel. *MusicLine* is the most well-rounded magazine both in editorial and in outreach. Retailers, radio programmers, concert promoters, and people involved in virtually every other aspect of the Christian music trade read this monthly publication. (This is starting to sound like a commercial, isn't it?) Also worth mentioning are those magazines which circulate primarily in the consumer sector. *Charisma, Christian Life, Campus Life, Cornerstone, Contemporary Christian Magazine, Spirit,* and *Group* are a few of them.

Begin to plan an ad campaign by asking yourself a few basic questions. Who is my audience for this record? How do I find these people? What is my budget? It is very important to decide which magazines reach the audience that your record is going to reach. It would be foolish to put an advertisement in *Campus Life* for a very traditional record that would appeal to a 40-year-old audience.

You can find out who reads the magazines by simply contacting each publishing company and asking for their media kit. You will usually receive a packet of very detailed information about the readership. Once you have this information, you can better decide which magazines you should advertise in. If your budget is limited (and whose isn't?), choose one or two magazines and place ads for several consecutive months rather than choosing several different magazines and running only once or twice in each. Repetition is one of the keys to successful advertising.

If you need help developing your ad campaign, contact the advertising directors of the various publications. They are very interested in selling you an ad and therefore can be very helpful in explaining how to create an ad. Also, the magazines have art departments that you can work with for a nominal cost.

You need to have an idea of what you want to communicate in the ad. Keep in mind, of course, the type of magazine you're running in. It's usually a good idea to have the ad run in a trade magazine a month or two ahead of the consumer magazines. (Remember, sell to the sellers!) An advance trade campaign enables retailers to have the records in place when your consumer campaign begins. You want to let them know that the album is available for distribution and how to get a hold of it. Let me mention that an ad in *MusicLine*, a magazine that's widely read by radio stations, can attract the attention of a lot of radio programmers as well as bookstore managers.

So what information should an ad include? Your ad should let the reader know who the artist is, what kind of music is contained on the album, and probably something (perhaps in the form of a testimonial or other intriguing copy) that will give the reader a good reason to find out more about your product. Above all, make sure that the ad tells the reader how to order the product.

In a consumer ad, the most important thing is information about the artist because people buy *artists* before they buy albums. Don't ever put anything in the ad that is going to detract from communicating who the artist is, what the record is, and how the readers can get it. While cute, clever concepts are nice, they are sometimes ineffective sales pieces. The name of the artist and the title of the album should virtually leap off the page at the reader. Don't forget that the main purpose of an ad is to sell the product and to create an awareness of it.

While the magazine's staff can help you structure your ad, remember that their business is selling space—not creating advertising materials for you. I would suggest that you find a good graphic artist in your area who can prepare advertising materials. You also need to be aware of the magazine's deadlines. Most publications close about two months before the issue date. Don't call up on August 15 expecting to get an ad in the September issue. Generally on August 15 you can't even get into the *October* issue!

CHAPTER TWENTY-ONE

Business Or Ministry

One's source of income, whatever it may be, is his occupation. That person's daily walk with the Lord and his interaction with others comprise his life and ministry. In many instances, our ministry will take place within the confines or actions of our occupations. Too often, though, we lump the two together in our own lives and in the lives of others. This distinction, however, is not a minor one. In fact, it brings into pinpoint focus the very issue of why we are doing what we're doing. Let me explain.

First, I am not saying that we shouldn't be Christians in our professional lives or that we can't minister during our business hours. I firmly believe that the Lord would have all of us be as honest and conscientious as possible in our business dealings. I also believe that He wants us to be giving, forgiving, and faithful in our daily walks. Our daily actions offer a far better witness to others than do our daily sermons!

Now let's consider the occupation of the "Christian artist." I often hear such disturbing comments as, "They're in it for the money" or "They're not walking their talk." But is it our place to wonder aloud about— much less judge—another brother's motives? Besides, mightn't these comments stem from a touch of jealousy over the fact that the Lord has blessed another in certain ways that we ourselves may not be blessed in?

More germane to the nuts and bolts of being a Christian artist is the issue of contracts. The occupation of "Christian artist" calls for dealing with agreements and contracts. While formal contracts between two Christians may seem unnecessary, the written statement will help prevent misunderstanding and bad feelings between members of the body. When I am finalizing a business agreement, I try to get everything in writing. That way, both parties have a written reminder of what each needs to do to fulfill that agreement. Contracts are very important *not* because of a lack of trust, but to serve as a clear statement of what was agreed to and as a reference point if one's memory is not what it could be.

If a gray area still arises, both parties should then ask the Lord for guidance and be sensitive to the answers He gives. As Christians, we all are called to keep our house and business affairs in order and to keep peace with everyone. I also believe that the Lord would have us be as accomplished and fair in business as possible and to take seriously a brother's request. In every decision, then, it is important that the search for God's will be our most primary goal.

Let me add at this point that we imperfect human beings may, on occasion, unintentionally break an agreement. Unintentionally doing someone wrong is obviously not right, but I believe we are really out of line when we fail to correct a wrong immediately once we become aware of it. I will never be able to do everything right, but I am always able to apologize and ask forgiveness for—and hopefully correct—my mistakes.

Another matter worth mentioning in this discussion of business and ministry is that of wages—of receiving an income from sharing the gospel in word, in print, or in song.

While even the idea of "making money off the gospel" is offensive to some people, the real issue is the heart—the motives—of the person who is preaching, singing, or writing. A person who spreads the Word primarily for financial reasons has not fooled the Lord for a moment. The Lord knows the heart and has the power to bless or limit a ministry. By the same token, the Lord knows the heart of those of us in the business who are involved because of a genuine love for Him and His people. He has the total authority to bless or not bless a person's ministry.

Scripture offers us various perspectives on the issue of receiving money when our occupation is also our ministry. First, hear 1 Corinthians 3:8—"He who plants and he who waters are equal, and each shall receive his wages according to his labor." Of those who are planting and watering out of less than pure motives, Matthew 7:16 says this: "Beware of false prophets... You will know them by their fruits." Finally, hear Paul's wise perspective on the different people who were sharing the gospel in his day: "Some indeed preach Christ from envy and rivalry, but others from good will. The latter do it out of love... The former proclaim Christ out of partisanship... What then? Only that in every way, whether in pretense or in truth, Christ is proclaimed; and *in that I rejoice*" (Philippians 1:15-18). If you are wrestling with the issue of income, go to God's Word for guidance and for peace.

Let me close with the reminder that we are not to judge one another's ministry. The Lord's chooses whom to bless. The Lord's also decides which methods to bless, and it is not our place to judge. Let us therefore guard our motives and our methods. And let us sincerely pray for the efforts of our brothers and sisters as they, in whatever way, seek to serve the same God with their talents. After all, we are all members of the same body of Christ Jesus.

CHAPTER TWENTY-TWO

A Note Of Encouragement

"Where do I start?" What a lonely, hopeless question! And if you feel that the Lord has a music ministry for you, you have probably asked that question and experienced those feelings. Where *do* you start? Again, in the beginning, the most important thing to do is to determine the type of ministry—local, regional, or national—to which you are called. While a national ministry has more widespread recognition, all ministries are equally important in the eyes of the Lord. Consider that an artist who sings in different cities each evening plants seeds in the hearts of those who hear, but rarely can this artist follow up with a new brother or sister in which the seed has taken root. On the other hand, an artist who is always in town has a greater opportunity to nurture the seeds sown in a concert. This artist would be available to help supply the spiritual food a young Christian needs to become firmly planted in God's Word.

Despite the advantages of local ministries, many people start out feeling that it's national or nothing. Certain signs, however, indicate when a national ministry is an unrealistic goal. If, for instance, you can't get any label interested in your album, if you can't get any of the songs played on a radio station other than your local station, and if you can't get anyone to record your songs, chances are that you should target your ministry to the local or regional audience. If the Lord chooses to widen your following, He can do so at any time. On the other hand, He may need you to remain right where you are for His purposes.

And let me say that a local ministry needn't be thought of as second-best. Consider the advantage of the availability that I mentioned earlier. Realize, too, that there's rarely ever a point that you can't make a full-time living at the local level of ministry. Neither should you conclude, "The Lord must not want me to be singing Christian songs anywhere, any time." You might decide to sing on a part-time basis. Play for church services, Christian banquets, and other local gatherings. If you touch even one person in all those appearances, it's worth continuing your ministry. It's important that all of us use the talents the Lord has given us. And the Lord doesn't say use them on a national basis. He says use them.

Furthermore, there's a genuine need for local ministries. Not everyone can or should have a national ministry, and those who do rarely, if ever, have an ongoing ministry at the local level. First of all, the national artists are not in their hometown long enough to be a consistent sounding board. They're usually on the road doing concerts or in the studio recording an album. Second, they can't stay in the cities they visit long enough to offer any significant follow-up on people they've prompted to think about their relationship with Christ. They perform one night and are gone the next day. People who attend these artists' concerts really do need an artist who's in town, an artist who's accessible, an artist who can answer the phone and talk about the questions a young believer has.

Let me therefore repeat myself. If you truly feel that you're called to some type of music ministry, don't give up on establishing a local ministry. If you've done everything you can to try to establish something at a regional or national level and nothing has worked, look objectively at your situation. Realize that the Lord may be calling you to a local ministry. Realize, too, that that calling doesn't make your ministry any less valid or any less vital. It just makes it local instead of national. I also firmly believe that He could be preparing you for a more widespread ministry, but He may be keeping the doors closed temporarily to prepare you for what's to come. It took two years from the start of Amy Grant's first album for it to be released, and I feel that the Lord was preparing her for what was to come. So never give up, but also don't try to force something that is not in the Lord's timing.

I can't emphasize too much that although a local artist may never sell truckloads of records or be on national television shows, the national artist may rarely be blessed with the opportunity to see the seeds he has planted in people grow into a faith that will stand firm. What is important is that we ask the Lord to use us in whatever place He calls us. Therefore, I want to encourage each of you to answer *your* calling and then to be the best you can be in that situation. Be thankful that you are a member of God's army fighting for the cause of the gospel. That cause—and there is none greater—is to bring lost souls to an awareness of Jesus Christ and His great sacrifice that gives us the opportunity to be seated for eternity at the right hand of God Almighty. What better purpose could there be on this earth?

While David with his harp is the best known, the Lord has used thousands for His glory through the ages. While David's songs have stood the test of time, thousands of other people's songs have lived on in the hearts and souls of the people they touched. You are as important a link in God's music ministry as the Shepherd-King David was. And with God's blessing, your songs can also live in other people's hearts for eternity. May God bless your desire and efforts to serve Him with your talent and in your life.

— Chris

Christian Radio Stations

KGFT, Tom Watson, 5565 Carpinteria N.E., Suite 24, Carpinteria, CA 98013

WJEP/AM 1020, Logan Whalen, P.O. Box 90, Thomasville, GA 31799

WCFY, Gary Gaskin, 108 Beck Lane, Lafayette, IN 47905

WKSJ/AM 1270, Tim O'Neil, P.O. Box 160706, Mobile, AL 36616

KERI/AM 1180, Fred Brakeman, Rt. 1, Box 38, Wasco, CA 93385

WYNX, Mark Niemand, 2460 Atlanta Rd., Smyrna, GA 30080

WBGL, Alan Kunkel, 2108 West Springfield, Champaign, IL 61821

WSAI, Jeff Eldred, 100 Commonwealth, Erlanger, KY 41018

KLYT, Rudy Grande, 3107 Eubank N.E., Scottsdale Village #19, Albuquerque, NM 87111

WGEV, Mike Nolt, Geneva College, Beaver Falls, PA 15010

WPRQ, Roger Chase, P.O. Box WPRQ, Kingsport, TN 37663

WNCM, Jim Knight, 2361 Cortez Rd., Jacksonville, FL 32216

WFEZ, Jim Bunn, P.O. Box 1414, Meridian, MS 39301

WHLO, Jim Robinson, 2650 W. Market St., Akron, OH 44313

KXOJ, Kim Harrison, P.O. Box 1250, Sapulpa, OK 74066

KJIA, Jeff Sauer, 305 W. 14th St., Sioux Falls, SD 57101

KLMB, David Graham, P.O. Box 21480, Shreveport, LA 71120-1480

WLFJ, Allen Henderson, 2420 Wade Hampton Blvd., Greenville, SC 29615

WFLT, Brian Mason, 317 S. Averill, Flint, MI 48506

WGWY, Bill Adkins, 1613 Lawrence Hwy., Charlotte, MI 48813

KOBC, Rob Kime, 1111 N. Main, Joplin, MO 64801

WKTX, Cles Holbrook, Mellon Bank Bldg, Suite 209-210, Mercer, PA 16137

WGSI, Corey Akeley, P.O. Box 434, Russell, PA 16345

KLTY, David Pierce, 2216 S. Cooper St., Arlington, TX 76013

WNLR, Mark Kender, P.O. Box 400, Churchville, VA 24421

WXRI, John Low, 1318 Sprately St., Portsmouth, VA 23705

WTIJ, John Krehbiel, Box 150, Waterbury, VT 05676

WKSH, Peter Howard, W223-N3251 Shady Ln., Pewaukee, WI 53072

WJYP, B.G. Hamrick, P.O. Box 8718, South Charleston, WV 25303

WWDJ, George Flores 167 Main Street Hackensack NJ 07602

WNNN, Patti Power, Box 132, Salem, NJ 08079

WLIX, Dave Koch, 138 West Main Street, Bay Shore, NY 11706

WSIV/WOIV, Chris Hauser, 7095 Myers Rd., East Syracuse, NY 13057

WJTL, Fred McNaughton, 780 Eden Rd., Lancaster, PA 17601

WZZD, Carl Dean, 117 Ridge Pike, LaFayette Hill, PA 19444

WCTN, Karen Lees, 7825 Tuckerman 21, Potomac, MD 20854

WTOW, Jeff Atherholt, 724 Delaney Valley Rd., Towson, MD 21204

WABS, Dawn Dicker, 5230 Lee Highway, Arlington, VA 22207

WKGM, Larry Cobb, Box 339, Smithfield, VA 23430

WBRG, John Abbott, Box 1079, Lynchburg, VA 24505

WBFJ, Steve Anderson, 3066 Trenwest Dr., Ste. A, Winston-Salem, NC 27103

WFOM, Jane Pedro, 835 South Cobb Drive, Marietta, GA 30060

WAEC, Beth Bailey, 1430 West Peachtree, Atlanta, GA 30309

WVFJ, Wayne Hagan, Box 510, Manchester, GA 31816

WHYD, Dave Kelly, 1825 Buena Vista, Columbus, GA 31906

WAPE, Steve Johnson, Box 486, Orange Park, FL 32073

WFSH, Kevin Wicker, P.O. Box 308, Valparaiso, FL 32580

WCIE, John Hull, 1350 East Main Street, Lakeland, FL 33801

WNDA, Mike Wilson, 2407 Ninth Ave., Huntsville, AL 35805

WASG, Randy Jeter, 1210 South Main Street, Atmore, AL 36502

WXLN, Doug Smith, 310 West Liberty, Louisville, KY 40202

WRFD, Bill DeWees, Box 802, Columbus, OH 43085

WGFT, Grace Lightner, 275 Federal Plaza, Youngstown, OH 44503

WTSJ, Chris Roberts, 602 Main Street, Cincinnati, OH 45202

WXIR, Phil Foley, 4802 East 62nd Street, Indianapolis, IN 46220

WHME, Craig Wallin, Box 12, South Bend, IN 46624

WYFC, Lou Velker, Box 1520, Ypsilanti, MI 48197

WWJO, Terry VanOss, 5658 143rd Street, Holland, MI 49423

WMAX, Don Melford, 3250 28th Street, S.E., Grand Rapids, MI 49508

KWKY, Cecil Van Houten, Box 662, Des Moines, IA 50303

KSAY, David Sasiela, Box 708, Clinton, IA 52732

KSLT, Gary Vesper, 745 Fifth Street, Spearfish, SD 57783

WEAW, Don Kiburz, 4320 Dundee Rd., Myrthbrook, ID 60062

WCRM, Jim Burkhart, 700 Willow Lane, Dundee, IL 60118

WCFL, Jim Channell, 300 North State Street, Chicago, IL 60618

WQFL, Ben Birdsong, 5257 Pebble Creek Trail, Rockford, IL 61111

WCIC, Lynn Marie, 3263 Court Street, Pekin, IL 61554

WCBW, Doug Smith, Box 147, Columbia, IL 62236

KLFJ, Don Burrell, 811 Booneville, Springfield, MO 65802

KCNW, Rita Frias, 4535 Metropolitan Ave., Kansas City, KS 66106

WSHO, Larry Alford, 4900 Veterans Memorial Blvd., Ste. 702, Metairie, LA 70003

KCFO, Brian Corea, 3737 S. 37th West Ave., Tulsa, OK 74107

KBBW, Matt Brandon, Box 2209, Waco, TX 76703

KGOL, Mike Perry, 8500-A Kirby, Houston, TX 77054

KSBJ, Mark Ryder, 200 CN Houston, Humble, TX 77338

KTFA, Frank Scales, Box 820, Bridge City, TX 77611

KIXL, Tom McDesmott, 1018 West llth Street, Austin, TX 78703

KGNZ, Kevin Grady, Box 2424, Abilene, TX 79504

KLTT, Roger Chapman, 2150 West 29th Street #200, Denver, CO 80211

KRDS, Mike Adams, 8611 North Black, Phoenix, AZ 85021

KNIS, Tim Allen, 6363 Hwy 50 East, Carson City, NV 89701

KYMS, Gem O'Brien, 1748 West Katella #106, Orange, CA 92667

KDAR, Brent Klein, 500 Esplanade Drive, Ste 1510, Oxnard, CA 93030

KTED, Tim Hulsey, 5755 East Kings Canyon, Fresno, CA 93727

KPDQ, Michael Carr, 5110 S.E. Stark Street, Portland, OR 97215

KCMS, Joe Michaels, 19303 Fremont Ave., Seattle, WA 98133

KLYN, Jim Bouma, 1843 Front Street, Lyden, WA 98264

Christian Studios

Adamo's Audio, 16571 Higgins Cr., Huntington Beach, CA 92647

Integrity Sound, 248 N. Broadway, Fresno, CA 93701

Mama Jo's, 8321 Lankershim Blvd., North Hollywood, CA 91605

Gold Mine Studio, 2020 Sunnyside Dr., Brentwood, TN 37027

MCA Whitney Recording Studio, Inc., 1516 W. Glenoaks Blvd., Glendale, CA 91201

Mixmasters Audio Production Specialists (formerly New World Recording), 4877 Mercury St., San Diego, CA 92111

Morning Star Sound Recorders, 4115 N. Maine, Baldwin Park, CA 91706

Poiema Studios, P.O. Box 651, Camarillo, CA 93010

Redhill Recording Studio, P.O. Box 238, La Mirada, CA 90637

Rose Studios, 1098 Rose Ave., El Centro, CA 92243

3-D Studios, 204 Cabrillo, Costa Mesa, CA 92627-3149

Weddington Studio, 11128 Weddington St., N. Hollywood, CA 91601

White Field Studios, Inc., 2902 W. Garry Ave., Santa Ana, CA 92704

Evan Williams Recording, 1519 S. Grand Ave., Santa Ana, CA 92706

Full Sail Recorders, 660 Douglas Ave., Altamonte Springs, FL 32701

London Music, Inc., 7120 N. Florida Ave., Tampa, FL 33604

The Sound Room, Inc., 325 Patterson Ave., Ft. Oglethorpe, GA 30742

Twelve Oaks Recording Studio, 3830 S. Cob Dr., Atlanta, GA 30080

Jor-Dan, Inc., 1100 Wheaton Oaks Ct., Wheaton, IL 60187-3043

Tone Zone Studio, 1316 N. Clibourn, Chicago, IL 60610

White Horse Recording, 620 15th St., Moline, IL 61265

Azi Productions, 1650 Cass St., Ft. Wayne, IN 46808

The Barn Recording Studio, P.O. Box 256, Alexandria, IN 46001

Pinebrook Recording Studios, Inc., P.O. Box 146, State Road #9 S., Alexandria, IN 46001-0146

Wieland Studios, 211 Fraser St., P.O. Box 573, Kawkawlin, MI 48631

Patmos Productions, 123 E. State St., Ridgeland, MS 39157

Kennett Sound Studios, Inc., P.O. Box 602, Kennett, MO 63857

Dream Maker Studios, 613 Powell Road, N.E., Lenoir, NC 28645

Ron King Productions, 208 Verona Dr., Washington, PA 15301

Mark Five, 10 Michael Dr., P.O. Box 7084, Greenville, SC 29610

Ardent Recordings, Inc., 2000 Madison Ave., Memphis, TN 38104

Bullett Recording Inc., 49 Music Square West, Nashville, TN 37203

The Music Box, P.O. Box 23645, Nashville, TN 37202

Brasswind Recording Studio, Ltd., 2551 Texas Ave., Shiloh Place, Suite F, College Station, TX 77840

Brian Sound Productions, Inc., P.O. Box 5587, Waco, TX 76708

Genesis Sound Studio (formerly Rainbow Sound Inc.), 1320 Inwood Rd., Dallas, TX 75247

Omega Audio, 8036 Aviation Pl., Dallas, TX 75235

Rivendell Recorders, 2223 Strawberry, Pasadena, TX 77502

Sound Arts, 914 Lake Air, Waco, TX 76710

Sierra Recording, 669 Seminary South, Ft. Worth, TX 76115

Sword & Shield Recording Co., 3301 Sublett Rd., P.O. Box 211, Arlington, TX 76016

Alive Recordings, 1251 Virginia Ave., Harrisonburg, VA 22801-1497

Triad Studios, 4572 150th Ave. N.E., Redmond, WA 98052

Sweetsong Productions/The Music Factory, P.O. Box 2041, Parkersburg, WA 26102

The Master's Workshop Corporation, 306 Rexdale Blvd., Unit 7, Rexdale (Toronto) Ontario, Canada M9W IR6

Christian Retailers

Mardel Warehouse, 5500 S.W. 36th, Oklahoma City, OK 73179

Baker Book House, 2768 E. Paris, S.E., Grand Rapids, MI 49506

Ft. Heritage Campground & Christian Retreat, Ft. Mill, SC 29715

One Way Book Shop #3, 4045 Union Road, Mehlville, MO 63129

Christian Publications, 315 West 43rd St., New York, NY 10036

Evangel, Inc., 127-106 Avenue, N.E., Bellevue, WA 98004

Berean Christian Bookstore, 441 Cleveland, Atlanta, GA 30315

Maranatha Christian Bookstore #2, 1190 Metrocenter "D", Jackson, MS 39209

Love Shop #12, 38 E. Hoover, Mesa, AZ 85202

Berean, 2465 Romig Road, Akron, OH 44320

Christian Book Dist., Inc., 137 Summit Street, Peabody, MA 01960

Good News Book Store, 7720 South University, Lubbock, TX 79423

Christian Book Center, 575 Soquel Avenue, Santa Cruz, CA 95062

Tree of Life, 1477 Roswell Road, Marietta, GA 30062

Lighthouse Christian Stores, 3000 Bellflower Blvd., Long Beach, CA 90808

United In Spirit, 4640 Park Blvd., Pinellas Park, FL 33565

Zondervan Family Bookstore, 3169 28th, S.E. Grand Rapids, MI 49508

Tampa Christian Supply Center, 208 W. Hillsboro, Tampa, FL 33614

Logos Bookstore, 716 West Grace St., Richmond, VA 23220

Western Book Tract, 2342 Monument Blvd., Pleasant Hill, CA 94523

Family Book Store, 4666 Fashion Square, Saginaw, MI 48603

Grand Bible Bookshop, 13731 Woodward, Highland Park, MI 48203

Jesus Chapel Book Store, 8029 E. Roosevelt, Scottsdale, AZ 85257

Mustard Seed, 150 E. Lancaster Avenue, Wayne, PA 19087

Family Life Center, 2055 Mt. Para, Atlanta, GA 30327

Zondervan Family Bookstore, Altamonte Mall Unit #889, Altamonte Springs, FL 32701

Zondervan Family Bookstore #90, 4201 Coldwater Road, Ft. Wayne, IN 46805

Lighthouse Christian Bookstore, 238 North Brand, Glendale, CA 91203

Zondervan Family Bookstore, 2101 South Lake Mall, Merrillville, IN 46410

Mustard Seed Christian Books, 2012 Auburn Ave., Box 12312, Columbus, GA 31906

Light & Life Bookstore, 4847 W. 38th Street, Indianapolis, IN 46254

Zondervan Family Bookstore, 3292C South Linden, Flint, MI 48507

Cornerstone, 9830-A Metro Parkway, East, Phoenix, AZ 85051

Christian Center Bookstore, 96 West Allendale Ave., Box 198, Allendale, NJ 07401

Christian Supply Shoppe, Inc., 303 East Wood Street, Spartanburg, SC 29303

New Horizons Bookshop, 6 Middle Country Road, Coram, NY 11727

Something More, 9733 W. Greenfield Avenue, West Allis, WI 53214

Lighthouse, 1545-B Cooper Hill, Birmingham, AL 35210

Zondervan Family Bookstore, 546 Jefferson Mall, Louisville, KY 40219

Maranatha Village, 2400 Sunflower Street, Santa Ana, CA 92704

Christian Supply Center, 10209 S.E. Division, Portland, Oregon

Provident Bookstore, 40 East King Street, Lancaster, PA 17602

Christian Armory Bible Bookstore, 2250 Morse Road, Columbus, Ohio 43229

Better Book Room, 358 North Main St. #3550, Wichita, KS 67201

Berean Church Supplies, 1100 30th N.W., Canton, OH 44709

Evangel Book Center, Inc., E 201 Boone Ave., Spokane, WA 99202

Dickson's Grand Bible Bookshop, 1315 South Woodward, Royal Oak, MI 48067

Berean Christian Music Ctr., 1557 Meridian Ave., San Jose, CA 95125

Joshua's Christian Discount Store, 5933 E. Rosedale, Ft. Worth, TX 76116

The Ark, 399 Federal Blvd., Denver, CO 80219

Carpenter Village, 415 West Southern, Tempe, AZ 85282

Fresno Bible House, 4750 North Blackstone, Fresno, CA 93726

Dightman's Bible Book Center, 3816 South Yakima, Tacoma, WA 98408

Zondervan Family Bookstore, 3407 Nicholasville, Lexington, KY 40503

Christian Corner, 250 North Lake Ave., Pasadena, CA 91101

Berean Christian Supply Ctr., 5035 North 35th Ave., Phoenix, AZ 85017

Heaven & Earth, 423 S. Lynnhaven Road, Suite 107, Virginia Beach, VA 23452

The Faithful Source, 50 Route 46 East Mt Lakes NJ 07046

Theophilus Bible Store, 5418 Bissonnet, Bellaire, TX 77401

Moody Bookstore, 845 North Wells Street, Chicago, IL 60610

Deeper Life Book Store, 12180 Garland Road, Dallas, TX 75218

Zondervan Family Bookstore, Richland Fashion Mall/MLSPl, Waco, TX 7671

Foothill Bible Book Store, 8227 La Mesa Blvd., La Mesa, CA 92041

Long's Christian Music Center, 2306 Edgewater Street, Orlando, FL 32804

Joy Bells Bible Book Store, 12932 Main Street, Garden Grove, CA 92640

Chapel Store, 3001 Sunflower Street, Santa Ana, CA 92704

Revelation Christian Book & Gift, Battlefield Mall, Springfield, MO 65804

Scripture Stall, 272 Wonderland St., San Antonio, TX 78201

Eden Books, 13705 Eureka Rd., Southgate, MI 48195

Berean Christian Book Store, 1078 San Antonio Dr., Colton, CA 92324

Bible Book Store, 2344 Grand Ave., Billings, MT 59102

Beardsley Book & Bible, 2221 McHenry Ave., Modesto, CA 95350

The Christian Armory, Inc., 3853-B Lawrenceville Hwy., Tucker, GA 30084

Provident Bookstore, Rts 113 & 39, Souderton, PA 18964

The Shepherd's Shoppe, 431 McCarthy, San Antonio, TX 78216

Spring Branch Bible & Bookstore, 613 Memorial City, Houston, TX 77024

The Living Word, 2268-C Wyoming, N.E., Albuquerque, NM 87112

Bender's Christian Supplies, 8550 Sheridan Drive, Williamsville, NY 14221

The Mustard Seed, Inc., 3139 S. Broadway, Englewood, CO 80110

Morgan's Book & Bible, 5116 196th St., Lynwood, WA 98036

Hackman's Bible Book Store, 1155 Mac Arthur Rd., Whitehall, PA 18052

Foothill Scripture House, 5353 Auburn, Sacramento, CA 95841

Agape Christian Bookstore, 570 College St., Jacksonville, FL 32204

Bible Book Store, 662 N.E. 125th Street, Miami, FL 33161

Puritan Reformed, 1319 Newport Gap, Wilmington, DE 19804

Berean Christian Book Center, 2619 Alta Arden Expressway, Sacramento, CA 95825

Berean Bookstore, 8436 Quadway St., Whittier, CA 90605

Valley Book & Bible Store, 6502 Van Nuys Blvd., Van Nuys, CA 91401

The Sign of the Fish, 5003 Falls of News, Raleigh, NC 27609

Fishers of Men, 8080 South Gessner, Houston, TX 77036

Berean Book Store, 3216 Ming Street, Bakersfield, CA 93304

Sonshine Shop, West Acres, Fargo, ND 58103

Gospel Supplies, 4508 East Broadway, Tucson, AZ 85711

Better Books Christian Center, 3500 South Broadway, Tyler, TX 75701

Dearborne Bible Book Store, 22481 Foothill Blvd., Hayward, CA 94541

Berean Bookstore, 9865 Montgomery Road, Cincinnati Ohio 45242

Ministries for Christ, 8557 Research Blvd., Austin, TX 78759

Family Book Store, 127 Monroeville, Monroeville, PA 15146

Jesus Book & Gift, 733 U.S Highway I, Iselin, NJ 08830

The Lord's Vineyard, 527 North Chelton, Colorado Springs, CO 80909

Christian Record Companies

Benson Records, 365 Great Circle Rd., Nashville, TN 37228

Christian Artists Records, P.O. Box 1990, Thousand Oaks, CA 91360

Home Sweet Home Records, P.O. Box 202406, Dallas, TX 75220

Light Records, P.O. Box 2222, Newbury Park, CA 91320

Maranatha! Music, P.O. Box 1396, Costa Mesa, CA 92626

Reunion Records, 120 30th Ave. N., Nashville, TN 37203

Sparrow Records, 9255 Deering Ave., Canoga Park, CA 91304

Starsong Records, 2223 Strawberry Village, Pasadena, TX 77502

Word Records, P.O. Box 1790, Waco, TX 76796

Word Records, P.O. Box 6900, Vancouver, BC V6B 4B5, Canada

Christian Song Publishing Companies

Ariose Music Group, 1103 8th Avenue South, Nashville, TN 37212

Benson Publishing Group, 365 Great Circle Drive, Nashville, TN 37228

C.A. Music, P.O. Box 1990, Thousand Oaks, CA 91360

The Eddie Crook Company, P.O. Box 213, Hendersonville, TN 37077

Home Sweet Home Music, P.O. Box 202406, Dallas, TX 75220

Lexicon Music, Inc., 3543 Old Conejo Road, #105, P.O. Box 2222, Newbury Park, CA 91320

Manna Music, P.O. Box 3257, Burbank, CA 91504

Maranatha! Music, 2902 West Garry, Santa Ana, CA 92704

Meadowgreen Music Inc., 8 Music Square West, Nashville, TN 37203

Singspiration Music, 1415 Lake Drive, S.E., Grand Rapids, MI 49506

Sparrow/Birdwing Music, 9255 Deering Ave., Chatsworth, CA 91311

Star Song Publishing Group, 2000 21st Avenue South, Nashville, TN 37212

Word Music, P.O. Box 1790, Waco, TX 76796

Christian Print Publishing Companies

Alexandria House, P.O. Box 300, Alexandria, IN 46001

The Benson Company, 365 Great Circle, Nashville, TN 37228

Brentwood Publishing, P.O. Box 1028, Brentwood, TN 37207

Broadman Press, 127 9th Avenue N., Nashville, TN 37234

C.A. Music, 3547 Old Conejo Road, Suite 101, Newbury Park, CA 91320

Doxology Music, Box M, Aiken, SC 29801

Glorysound, 1 Waring Drive, Delaware Water Gap, PA 18327

Good Life Publications, Inc., 3901 Airport Freeway, Suite 200, Bedford, TX 76021

Gospel Publishing House (Melody Music), 1445 Boonville Ave., Springfield, MO 65802

Hinshaw Music, P.O. Box 470, Chapel Hill, NC 27514

Jenson Publications, 2770 S. 171st Street, New Berlin, WI 53151

Lexicon Music Inc., P.O. Box 2222, Newbury Park, CA 91320

Lillenas Publishing Co., P.O. Box 527, Kansas City, MO 64141

Lorenz Creative Services, 40 Music Square East, Nashville, TN 37203

Manna Music, Inc., 2111 Kenmere Avenue, Burbank, CA 91504

Psalm 150 Publications, 550 Lively, San Antonio, TX 78213

Purifoy Publishing Co., P.O. Box 31057, Knoxville, TN 37930

Robinsong Publishing Co., P.O. Box 1316, Marshall, TX 75671

Servant Publications, 840 Airport Blvd., Ann Arbor, MI 48197

Singspiration, Division of the Zondervan Corporation, 1415 Lake Drive SE, Grand Rapids, MI 49506

Sparrow/Birdwing Music, 9255 Deering Avenue, Chatsworth, CA 91311

Word Music, P.O. Box 1790, Waco, TX 76796

Christian Booking Agents

Accolade Productions, P.O. Box 121, West Middleton, IN 46995

Agape Force, P.O. Box 386, Lindale, TX 75771

Airborn Concert Control, P.O. Box 3064, Flint, MI 48502

BTA Ministries, P.O. Box 158542, Nashville, TN 37215

Bell, Mark, 3661 Airport Blvd. #95, Mobile, CA 36608

Bendett Artist Agency, David, 2431 Briarcrest Rd., Beverly Hills, CA 90210

Birdsong Agency, 2714 Westwood Dr., Nashville, TN 37204

Blackwood Prod., Ron Blackwood, P.O. Box 17272, Memphis, TN 38187-0272

Blanton & Harrell, 120 30th Ave. N., Nashville, TN 37203

Booking Agency, The, P.O. Box 120713, Nashville, TN 37212

Brother of the Son, P.O. Box 186, Crested Butte, CO 81224

Burkhart/Abrams/Michaels/Douglas, 6500 River Chase Cr. E., Atlanta, GA 30328

Calvary Music Group, 142 Eighth Ave. North, Nashville, TN 37203

Cavale Artists, 913 W. Center, Visalia, CA 93291

Century II Productions, P.O. Box 22707, Nashville, TN 37202

Chalace Music, P.O. Box 1542, Tacoma, WA 98401

Christian Artists Concert Mgt., 57 Tuxedo Rd., Montclair, NJ 07042

Christian Concert Artists, P.O. Box 9176, Fort Lauderdale, FL 33310

Christian Concerts Unlimited, 2901 Columbus, Ft. Worth, TX 76106

Christian Artists, Box 1984, Thousand Oaks, CA 91360

Come Alive Ministries, P.O. Box 86, Medford, NJ 08055

Continental Sound, Postbus 81065, Rotterdam, Holland

Coombs Agency, Wayne, 75 Malaga Cove Plaza, Palos Verdes Es., CA 90274

Cornerstone Prod., 3909 South Blvd., Suite 228, Charlotte, NC 28209

Coulter & Assoc., Tim, P.O. Box 28097, Columbus, OH 43228-0097

Creative Artists, Box 14543, Oklahoma City, OK 73113

D.C. Associates, 9754 Cedar St., Cypress, CA 90639

David Brown, W. 915 2nd Ave., Spokane, WA 99204

Desert Paradise Agency, P.O Box 26015, Colorado Springs, CO 80936

Dev-Song Scheduling, P.O. Box 1922, Lancaster, CA 93539

Don Light Talent, 1100 17th Ave. S., Nashville, TN 37212

Dusk & Dawn Productions/Records, 1810 Elton Road, Adelphi, MD 20783

El-Most Productions, Box 41291, Dallas, TX 75241

Evy-Pollen, Eric James, Box 323, Chiloquin, OR 97624

Firewind Artist Agency, 16439 Middle Beach Road, White Rock, BC V4B 5A8, Canada

Fletcher Christianson Prom., R.D. #1 Box 79-B, Roaring Spring, PA 16673

Gaub Ministries, Ken, Box 1, Yakima, WA 98907

Gold Street Agency, P.O. Box 75, Belmont Hills, PA 19004

Good Companies, 5519 W. Martin Dr. #10, Milwaukee, WI 53208

Great Gospel Agency, 1719 West End Ave., Nashville, TN 37203

Greg Menza Artists, 2055 Mt. Paran Rd. NW, Atlanta, GA 30327

Grimnes, Mike, P.O. Drawer 59808, Birmingham, AL 35259

Harrison & Asso, Tom, 105 Oak Valley Dr., Nashville, TN 37207

Harvest Ministries, P.O. Box 411, Lindale, TX 75771

Heartland Artists, 660 Douglas Ave., Altamonte Springs, FL 32714

Helvering Agency, 530 Grand Avenue, Anderson, IN 46012

Holmes Agency, 2008 S. Yale, Suite F, Santa Ana, CA 92704

J.C. Enterprises, P.O. Box 512, Randolph, MA 02368-0512

Jesus Unlimited Productions, 1043 Jacques Ave., Rahway, NJ 07065

Justus Productions, P.O. Box 204, Avondale Est., GA 30002

King, Ron, 208 Verona Drive, Washington, PA 15301

Landis Agency, P.O. Box 100512, Nashville, TN 37210

LeFevra Productions, P.O. Box 11766, Fort Wayne, IN 46860

Linda Miller & Associates, P.O. Box 531, Brentwood, TN 37027

Little Dixie, P.O. Box 1181, Florissant, MO 63031

Logsdon Associates, P.O. Box 137, New Providence, PA 17560

Lord & Roberts Productions, P.O. Box 241024, Memphis, TN 38124

Lori White, 2806 Lorraine Ave., Tampa FL 33614

MTD Artists Agency, Hans Altena, Box 7452, Grand Rapids, MI 49510

Manna Music, 2111 Kenmore, Burbank, CA 91504

Maranatha! Music, P.O. Box 1396, Costa Mesa, CA 92654

Masterpeace Arts, P.O. Box 321, Eureka Springs, AR 72632

Masterpiece & MPM Productions, P.O. Box 727, Sunnymead, CA 92388

Mays, Diane, P.O. Box 17858, Nashville, TN 37217

McKinney, Michael & Associates, P.O. Box 5162, Louisville, KY 40205

McKinnon, Kathy, P.O. Box 22700, Memphis, TN 38122

Messianic Booking Agency, 7708 City Line Ave., Philadelphia, PA 19151

Ministry Resource Center, P.O. Box 1396, Costa Mesa, CA 92628

Mission Control, 560 Revolutionary Way, Warminster, PA 18974

Mt. Moriah, P.O. Box 100, Lindale, TX 75771

Music Management Inc., P.O. Box 3533, Flint, MI 48502

New Creation Min., 12013 76th St. #202, Edmonton, Alta. T5B 2C9, Canada

New Direction Artists Guild, P.O. Box 50, Nashville, TN 37020

New Life Productions, Terry Scott, 1611 Riverside Dr., #24, Tulsa, OK 74119

New Song Ministry, 1507 Childs St., Tallahassee, FL 32303

North American Liturgy Resources, 10802 N. 23rd Ave., Phoenix, AZ 85029

PC Associates, P.O. Box 175, Ft. Wayne, IN 46801

Painter, R.A. & Associates, 112 Essex Ave., 30-C, Altamonte, FL 32701

Paradise Group, P.O. Box 25325, Nashville, TN 37202

Paul Jenkinson Agency, P.O. Box 669, Wilderville, OR 97543

Peaceable, 3525 Encinal Canyon Rd., Malibu, CA 90265

Pisteno Enterprises, 6162 E. Mockingbird, Dallas, TX 75214

Poiema Music, 506 Cottonwood St., Woodland, CA 95695

Praise Artists Mgt., 13841 Redhill #35 Tustin, CA 92680

Regency Artists, 9200 Sunset Blvd., #823, Los Angeles, CA 90069

Retreat Resource Group, John Van Dersall, P.O. Box 616, Navarre, OH 44662

Ron Cotnam & Associates, P.O. Box 4436, Ft. Worth, TX 76106

Sangre Productions, 9844 Business Park Dr., Sacramento, CA 95827

Seeds Incorporation, Box 220601, Charlotte, NC 28222

Shekinah Artists Agency, P.O. Box 380582, San Antonio, TX 78280

Signature Artists, Piry Wylie, 14874 88 "A" Avenue, Surrey, BC V3R 7T3, Canada

Solid Rock Agency, 1482 De Tracey St., San Jose, CA 95128

Solid Rock Ministry, 88 Bergen Tpke., Ridgefield Park, NJ 07660

Son-Key, P.O. Box 31757, Aurora, CO 80041

Songchild Prod., #8 Heather Place, Route #2, Washington, VA 26181

Speer Office, Speer Office, 54 Music Square W., Nashville, TN 37202

Splendor Productions, P.O. Box 1776, Longwood, FL 32750

Street Level Artists, 32 S. Raymond Ave., Ste. 8, Pasadena, CA 91105

Subrena Artists, 1650 Broadway, Suite 410, New York, NY 10019

Sunbelt Group, 2000 21st Ave. S., Nashville, TN 37212

Tatom Agency, 6750 W. 75th, 2A, Overland Park, KS 66204

Taylor Ministries, P.O. Box 523, Galena Park, TX 77547

Teen Challenge, Box 98, Rehresburg, PA 19550

Terry Cox Artist Agency, P.O. Box 40304, Nashville, TN 37204

Tom McBee Promotions, 50 Music Square W., Nashville, TN 37203

Tone Zone Agency, 4707 N. Malden, Chicago, IL 60640

Visions West Talent, 9350 Wilshire Blvd. #201, Beverly Hills, CA 90212

Wakeup Promotions, 194 Ripplewood Dr., Rochester, NY 14616

Christian Image, P.O. Box 91148, Mobile, AL 36608

Christian Festivals

Camp Meeting '84, Carrier Dome, P.O. Box 4981, Syracuse, NY 13202

Christian Artists Europe, Box 81137, Rotterdam, 3009 GC, Holland

Christian Artists, P.O. Box 1984, Thousand Oaks, CA 91360

Creation, P.O. Box 86, Medford, NJ 08055

Discoverry Festival, 1006 Ashville Highway, Brevard, NC 28712

Exodus '84, Laurel Hills Ranch, Victoria, TX

Fall Festival, Wings of Faith, P.O. Box 2590, El Cajon, CA 92021

Fall Festival Music Convention, Wings of Faith, P.O. Box 2590, El Cajon, CA 92021

Fishnet, P.O. Box 1919, Front Royal, VA 22630-1919

Floodstage, 410 Garsche, Collinsville, IL 62234

Jesus Challenge '84, Harold Zimmeman, Wabash Rd. R.D.. #1, Ephrata, PA 17522

Jesus Hawaii 84, P.O. Box 89543, Honolulu, HI 96830

Jesus Northwest, P.O. Box 7718, Salem, OR 97303

Jesus Texas Festival, P.O. Box 41291, Dallas, TX 75241

Jesus in 84, Faith Fellowship of Ohio, P.O. Box 152, Vincent, OH 45784

Music City Song Festival, 1014 16th Ave. South, Nashville, TN 37212

National Quartet Convention, 54 Music Square West, Nashville, TN 37203

Natl' Christian Youth Congress, P.O. Box 481, Loveland, CO 80537

Praise Unto Jesus, Box 137, Blanchard, MI 49310

Resurrection Festival, P.O. Box 8490, Madison, WI 53716

Son Shine 84, P.O. Box 1444, Willmar, MN 56201

Texas Jesus Crusade, Box 41291, Dallas, TX 75241

Western Deserts Gospel Sing, P.O. Box 351, Apple Valley, CA 92307

Christian Organizations

Artists in Christian Testimony, 9090 19th St., Alta Loma, CA 91701

Christian Artists Int'l, P.O. Box 2134, Lynnwood, WA 98036

Colorado Arts, and Music Fellowship, P.O. Box 10810, Denver, CO 80210

Continental Sound, Postbus 81065, Rotterdam, 3009 GB, Holland

Evangelical Press Assoc. Inc., Box 4559, Overland Park, KS 66204

Fellowship of Contemporary Christian Ministries, P.O. Box 928, Adrian, MI 49221

Fellowship of Christian Musicians, Bill Anderson, 3100 Fleetwood, B-7, Amarillo, TX 79109

Michigan Cont. Christian Min. (MCCM), c/o Shelter, 204 Butler St., Clio, MI 48420

Ministry Resource Center, P.O. Box 1396, Costa Mesa, CA 92626

Missions (Europe), YWAM, 50 Prins Hendrikkade, 1012 Amsterdam, Holland

Religion In Media, 6817 Franklin Ave., Los Angeles, CA 90028

Teen Challenge Training Center, Rehresburg, PA 19550

The Artist Guild, P.O. Box 1520, Grand Rapids, MI
Vineyard Arts Fellowship, P.O. Box 7816, Atlanta,
GA 30309

Christian Periodicals

Bookstore Journal, 2620 Venetucci Blvd., P.O. Box 200, Colorado Springs, CO 80901

Buzz, 37 Elm Road, New Malden, KT3 3HB, England

Campus Life, 400 E. St. Charles Rd., Carol Stream, IL 60187

Cash Box, 1775 Broadway, New York, NY 10019

Charisma, 174 W. Comstock Ave., Suite 100, Winter Park, FL 32789

Christian Activities Calendar, P.O. Box 3340, Laguna Hills, CA 92654

Christian Music Today, Celebration Concerts, P.O. Box 1903, Fremont, CA 94538

Christian Bookseller, 396 E. St. Charles Rd., Wheaton, IL 60188

Christian Courier, P.O. Drawer 1405, Apple Valley, CA 92307

Contemporary Christian Magazine, P.O. Box 6300, Laguna Hills, CA 02654

Cornerstone, 4704 N. Malden, Chicago, IL 60640

Cornerstone Gospel News, P.O. Box 365, Franklin, OH 45005

Creator, No. 25 Rolling Hills Dr., Wichita, KS 67212

Dr. Redempto's Rock Report, P.O. Box 1524, Blaine, WA 98230

Encore, P.O. Box 10876, Oklahoma City, OK 73140

FCCM Newsletter, Fellowship Cont. Christian Min., P.O. Box 928, Adrian, MI 49221

Faith In Action, Ken Gaub, P.O. Box 1, Yakima, WA 98907

Gospel Music Magazine, Postbus 81065, Rotterdam, 3009 GB, Holland

Gospel Rama News, P.O. Box 6617, Washington D.C., 20009

Group, 425 E. Eisenhower Box 481, Loveland, CO 80539

In Tune, P.O. Box 640, Grapevine, TX 76051

Modern Liturgy, 7291 Coronado Drive, San Jose, CA 95129

Motif Magazine, 17 N. State, Suite 1222, Chicago, IL 60602

New Christian Music, 46 Alexandra Crescent, Kent, BR1 4EU, England

MusicLine, P.O. Box 6300, Laguna Hills, CA 92654

Performance, 1020 Currie St., Fort Worth, TX 76107

Progressive Pacer Production Inc., Box 8363, St. Paul, MN 55113

Religious Broadcasting, 101 New Maple Ave., Pine Brook, NJ 07058

Revelations Chronicles, 945 N. 7th St , Terre Haute, IN 47807

Scan, P.O. Box 12811, Pittsburgh, PA 15241

Singing News, P.O. Box 5188, Pensacola, FL 32505

Twin Cities Christian, 1619 Portland Ave. S., Minneapolis, MN 55404

Christian Promoters

Accolade Productions, P.O. Box 121, West Middleton, IN 46995

Airborne Productions, P.O. Box 8054, Chattanooga, TN 37411

Alternative Music Association, 2543 37th Ave. S., Minneapolis, MN 55406

Andes, Larry, P.O. Box 1919, Front Royal, VA 22630

Brallier Productions, P.O. Box 24057, Nashville, TN 37202

CLM Promotions, Ronald Boswel, 7712 Faircrown Dr., San Antonio, TX 78242

Carlson, Rusty, 132 Czeck Hall Pl., Yukon, OK 73099

Celebration Concerts, Jon Robberson, P.O. Box 1903, Fremont, CA 94538

Chariot Productions, #203 12231A Fort Road, Edmonton, AL T5B 4H2, Canada

Charisma Latina Prod., P.O. Box 21192, Phoenix, AZ 85036

Christian Concert Series, Jim Gabriels, Chairman, P.O. Box 961, Sheboygan, WI 52081

Christian Concerts Unlimited, P.O. Box 4436 Ft. Worth, TX 76106

Come Alive Min., Box 86, Medford, NJ 08055

Continental Sound, Postbus 81065, Rotterdam, 3009 GB, Holland

Cornerstone Concerts, P.O. Box 707, Newcomb Hall, Charlottsville, VA 22901

Cornerstone Prod., P.O. Box 605, Champaign, IL 61820

Creation, P.O. Box 1573, Lancaster, PA 17603

Creative Concerts, P.O. Box 14543, Oklahoma City, OK 73113

Dusk & Dawn Productions, 1810 Elton Rd., Adelphi, MD 20783

Eagle Productions, P.O. Box 243, Ravena, NY 12143-0243

Encore Productions, Inc., P.O. Box 38, Roseville, MI 48066-0080

Faith Ministry, Jim Edwards, 2536 East 4th, Tulsa, OK 74104

Garland & Assoc., Terry, P.O. Box 1648, Portland OR 97207

Give God the Glory, Box 41291, Dallas, TX 75241

Good Companies, 5519 W. Martin Dr. #10, Milwaukee, WI 53208

Harvest Productions, 100 E. Chicago St. #1404, Elgin, IL 60120

Hinkle, Scott P., 3571 Ruffin Rd. #247, San Diego, CA 92123

ICM, 928 Carpinteria St., Ste. 8, Santa Barbara, CA 93103

J.C. Enterprises, P.O. Box 512, Randolph, MA 02368-0512

Jesus Christ Unlimited, Jo Stern, Rte. 1, Box 483, St. Albans, WV 25177

Jesus Christ Unlimited, Min. Inc., 5175 Big Tyler Rd., Charleston, WV 25313

Jesus Northwest, Rod Chandler, P.O. Box 7718, Salem, OR 97303

Johnson, Byron J.D.C. Promotions, 2651 La Cienega Ave., Los Angeles, CA 90034

King, Ron Promotions, 208 Verona Drive, Washington, PA 15301

Lighthouse Christian Ministries, Centre Rd. & Gilpin Dr., Wilmington, DE 19805

Living Water Mini., CJ Caler, 606 Queens, Pasadena, TX 77502

Lord & Roberts Productions, P.O. Box 241024, Memphis, TN 38124

Matthews Music Min., P.O. Box 111593, Nashville, TN 37211

Men of Harmony, P.O. Box 961, Sheboygan, WS 53081

Midnight Son Productions, Outreach Unlimited, P.O. Box 562, Toledo, OH 43693

Morning Star, Inc., 907 Eicher, Springdale, AR 72764

Music Management Inc., P.O. Box 3533, Flint, MI 48502

New Covenant Productions, Mike Clark, 202 South East St., Plainfield, IN 46168

New Harvest Promotions, Dale S. Wolfe, P.O. Box 3-307 ECB, Anchorage, AK 99501

New Life Productions, Cannon Community Church, P.O. Box 454, Cannon Falls, MN 55009

New Song Ministry, 1507 Childs St., Tallahassee, FL 32303

Olson, Roger, Madison Gospel Tabernacle, 4909 E. Buckeye Rd., Madison, WI 53716

Outreach Concerts, 5433 Apple Drive, Ft. Collins, CO 80526

Parker, Lloyd, WLIX, 138 W. Main St., Bayshore, NY 11706

Perkins, Dan, Kingdom Productions, P.O. Box 18154, Shreveport, LA 71138

Pierce, Jay J., A Sound Ministry, 10012 N. Dale Mabry #208, Tampa, FL 33618

Praise Him Promotion, Mr. Craig Jordan, 27 Grassington Crescent, Scarborough, Ont. M1G 1X4, Canada

Progressive Pacer Prod., Inc., Box 8363, St. Paul MN 55113

Promises Concerts, 12131 Florida Blvd., Baton Rouge, LA 70815

Rainbow Productions, 1333 S. Smith, West St. Paul, MN 55118

Red Squirrel Flying, Inc., P.O. Box 1524, Blaine, WA 98230

Road Home Management, P.O. Box 10810, Denver, CO 80210

Shekinah Inc., P.O. Box 203, Callahan, FL 32011

Songchild Prod., #8 Heather Place, Rt. 2, Washington, VA 26181

Spring House Association, Inc., Box 178, Alexandria, IN 46001

Strait Gate Productions, P.O. Box 928, Adrian, MI 49221

Susquehanna Sound, 48 A Street, Northumberland, PA 17857

The Real Thing, Inc., R.R. #2 Box 73 B, Brighton, IA 52540

The Sound Dept. Inc., 705 Gasche St., Wooster, OH 44691

Thrasher, Tom, Christian Music, 10125-227th Ave. CT.E., Buckley, WA 98321

Truth Minitries, R.R. 3 Box 170, Chatfield, MN 55923

Truth Productions, 1178 Chesapeake Bay, Palatine, IL 60067

Under the Sun, P.O. Box 264, Archbold, OH 43502

VMS Production, c/o Charles T. Murphy, P.O. Box 1946, Logan WV 25601

Wakeup Promotions, 194 Ripplewood Dr., Rochester, NY 14616

Wings of Faith, P.O. Box 2590, El Cajon, CA 92021

YAM, Inc., P.O. Box 2032, Kalamazoo, MI 49003

About The Author

Chris Christian is an artist, songwriter, top ten record producer, record producer, record company president, and a multi-talented instrumentalist.

As a songwriter Chris has written for Elvis Presley, Dionne Warwick, Olivia Newton-John, Sheena Easton, Amy Grant, B.J. Thomas, the Carpenters, the Imperials, plus many more.

He has produced or executive produced over 100 albums, four of which won Grammys, with eight being nominated.

Chris is also a pioneer in the contemporary Christian music industry. He has won three Dove awards and produced albums for such artists as: Amy Grant, Steve Archer, B.J. Thomas, Imperials, the Boone Girls, Luke Garrett, among others.

He has also been responsible for starting the careers of Amy Grant, Whiteheart, David Martin, Rick Riso, Luke Garrett, Dogwood and Fireworks.

Additional Contributors include:
- Jack Joseph Puig, Engineer/Producer.
- Nathon Bart, Bass Player.
- Jeremy Dalton, Songwriter.
- Dann Huff, Guitar Player.
- Rhonda Jesson, Album Cover Designer.

To order extra copies of this book see your local Christian bookstore or send $12.95 plus $3.00 for shipping and handling to:

Home Sweet Home Publications Inc.
P.O. Box 202406
Dallas, TX 75220